Inspired by
Thomas Hardy

An Anthology of Students' Poems
Inspired by Reading Thomas Hardy

2019

Inspired by
Thomas Hardy

An Anthology of Students' Poems
Inspired by Reading Thomas Hardy

2019

Edited by Faysal Mikdadi

Roving
Press

Step-Up Books

© 2019 The Thomas Hardy Society
Published by Roving Press Ltd under the Step-Up Books imprint
4 Southover Cottages, Frampton, Dorset, DT2 9NQ, UK
Tel: +44 (0)1300 321531, www.rovingpress.co.uk

Distributed by The Thomas Hardy Society
c/o Dorset County Museum, Dorchester, Dorset DT1 1XA
Tel: +44 (0)1305 251501
E-mail: info@hardysociety.org
www.hardysociety.org

First published 2019 by Roving Press Ltd

ISBN: 978-1-906651-350

British Library Cataloguing in Publication Data
A catalogue record for this book is available from the British Library

Set in 11.5/13 pt Minion by Beamreach Printing (www.beamreachuk.co.uk)
Printed and bound in England by Beamreach Printing

Contents

Dorchester Middle School

Greenwood Academy

St Ives School

St Osmund's Church of England Middle School

The Taunton Academy

The Thomas Hardye School

Trewirgie Junior School

Acknowledgements

Go find it, faeries, go and find
That tiny pinch of priceless dust,
And bring a casket silver-lined,
And framed of gold that gems encrust;

And we will lay it safe therein,
And consecrate it to endless time;
For it inspired a bard to win
Ecstatic heights in thought and rhyme.

from *Shelley's Skylark*
Thomas Hardy

A very large number of people were involved in these Thomas Hardy Poetry Workshops which took place between January and June 2019. Slightly over one hundred students were involved in reading, discussing and emulating Hardy's poetry. To them alone goes the credit for all that is beautiful in this Anthology.

This Anthology would not have been possible without the support of the participants' parents who kindly allowed their children to take part in the Thomas Hardy Poetry Workshops and who also gave permission for their children's poems to be published.

Sincerest gratitude goes to the many colleagues in the nine schools whose students took part in the Workshops. Bryanston School: Nick Kelly (Teacher of English), Emma Minter (Chartered Librarian), Sarah Thomas (Headteacher) and Emily Weatherby (Head of English). Cape Cornwall School: Sarah Crawley (Headteacher), Olga Keith (PA to the Leadership Team), Catherine Lawry (Mathematics Teacher and Student Voice Co-ordinator), Kellie Rushbury (Director of Learning) and Becky Watkins (Receptionist). Dorchester Middle School: Caroline Dearden (Headteacher) and Rob Murray (Faculty Lead for English). Greenwood Academy: Alan Bird (Headteacher) and Charlotte Hammond (Head of English). St Ives School: Cherie Bayfield (PA to the Headteacher),

Jonathan Hall (Assistant Headteacher – Innovation and Effectiveness), Cuedda Proudfoot-Taylor (Teacher of English) and Jan Woodhouse (Headteacher of St Ives and Executive Headteacher at Cape Cornwall). St Osmund's Church of England Middle School: Anna February-Perring (Year 7 Tutor) and Saira Sawtell (Headteacher). Taunton Academy: Rachael Logsdon (Deputy Head of Faculty – English, Literacy and Media) and Jen Veal (Headteacher). Thomas Hardye School: Mike Foley (Headteacher) and Rachel Glennie (Head of English). Trewirgie Junior School: Michelle Burton (Office Manager), Jane Sargent (Headteacher), Mhairi Saville (Curriculum Lead and Year 5 Teacher) and Dan Simons (Deputy Headteacher).

Mrs Rachel White, headteacher of Bishop's Hull Primary School in Taunton kindly gave her support for the publication of school pupil Lydia Martin's Thomas Hardy Victorian Fair poem.

A helpline adviser of the Department for Education (DfE) was very helpful in answering queries regarding issues of compliance with the General Data Protection Regulation (GDPR). She patiently checked on data privacy with two colleagues to ensure that this Anthology was GDPR compliant.

There were several persons outside the schools visited whose help and support were gratefully received. The National Trust generously welcomed the Taunton Academy young poets to Max Gate on Friday 7 June 2019. The Trust also ran the Thomas Hardy Young Poetry Prize 2019 and gave permission for the six finalists' entries to be published in this Anthology. Gratitude goes to the following colleagues from the National Trust: Michelle Caesar (Visiting Experience Officer), Elizabeth Flight (Assistant Business Support Co-ordinator), Hannah Jefferson (General Manager), Rebecca Paveley (Senior Marketing and Communications) and Martin Steven (Visitor Experience Manager).

Thanks also go to Dr Catherine Charlwood, Andrew Hewitt and Dr Karin Koehler for including a poetry reading and writing slot in their 'Writing about illness and well-being in the nineteenth century' Students' Day Programme. This day was part of the overall educational outreach programme for teachers and students included in the University of Oxford's 'Diseases of Modern Life'. Students spent the session responding creatively to nineteenth-century concerns about illness and well-being by writing their own poems after reading Hardy's 'An August Midnight' and two short extracts from Charles Darwin's The Origin of Species and The Descent of Man. Extension work was also given to students to take away and respond to in their own time. The works presented were Hardy's 'The Voice' and a short extract from Mary Wollstonecraft's *A Vindication of the Rights of Women.*

Gratitude is due to many more colleagues who helped in different ways: Virginia Astley was instrumental in judging the entries for the National Trust Thomas Hardy Poetry Competition 2019; Maggie Hoyle and Susan Walpole suggested the title finally adopted for this Anthology; Andrew Munro supported and encouraged the Poetry Workshop at Max Gate; Julie Musk of Roving Press patiently offered invaluable advice all through the process of production; Professor Angelique Richardson of the University of Exeter was generous with her encouragement and advice in ways too many to list here including during her part in judging the entries for the National Trust Thomas Hardy Poetry Competition 2019; Catherine D. Walker, Managing Director of Sprint in Dorchester, was generous with her time in producing the necessary resources to run the Workshops. On Sunday 2 June 2019, Sue Worth kindly stepped in at the last minute to read the finalists' poems in the National Trust Thomas Hardy Poetry Competition 2019 at Max Gate.

Thanks are also due to the Members of The Thomas Hardy Society Council of Management for their unstinting support and encouragement all through the academic year 2018–2019.

Members of the Dorchester Thomas Hardy Poetry Group shared their love and understanding of Hardy's poetry in a way that influenced the poems selected for the Workshops. They also took a great interest in the young poets' compositions, some of which were shared with them at various points of the year.

The Cape Cornwall Golf & Leisure in St Just in Cornwall and the Holiday Inn Express Hotel in Birmingham both allowed a small discount upon hearing that the Thomas Hardy Poetry Workshops were run by the Registered Charity The Thomas Hardy Society.

Finally, whilst every effort has been made to acknowledge all those kind persons who helped in so many ways in making this Anthology possible, if there has been any omission at all, there is no discourtesy intended. If such an omission has been made, or if any reader spots any error in this publication, please contact The Thomas Hardy Society and a correction will be issued in future publications. A brief e-mail to info@hardysociety.org will be gratefully received and promptly dealt with.

Preface

This Anthology includes all the 134 poems submitted by students from the nine schools that took part in the Thomas Hardy Poetry Workshops from January to June 2019. The poems include the six finalists' compositions from entries for the National Trust Thomas Hardy Young Poetry Prize 2019 as well as Lydia Martin's poem written during her visit to the Thomas Hardy Victorian Fair on Sunday 2 June 2019.

All poems are presented precisely as they were submitted by the young poets who were promised that their voice would be respected. They were also given the following three principles underlying all the Workshops:

1. 'There is no good poetry or bad poetry: there is only self-expression within a free and mutually supportive group.'
2. 'Composing a poem could be quite artificial and does not need a muse to propel the poet forward.'
3. 'Poets can take whatever liberties they wish in using poetic licence when adapting, rewriting or borrowing from Thomas Hardy's poems.' (See 'Afterword' and 'Appendix 2' for more details.)

Any amendments to the poems published here were made by the students as a result of discussions amongst their group. Apart from taking part in the discussions of Hardy's and the students' poems, adults present did not interfere with the processes of composition. Glaring errors were pointed out and left to the students to amend or leave if they deemed the 'error' as being part of the individual poet's original intent.

Faysal Mikdadi
Academic Director of The Thomas Hardy Society
Dorchester

National Trust Thomas Hardy Young Poetry Prize 2019

The National Trust Thomas Hardy Young Poetry Prize 2019 was open to entries from 13–18 year olds who lived or went to school in Dorset.

The Judges were Virginia Astley (musician and writer), Professor Angelique Richardson (University of Exeter) and Faysal Mikdadi (Academic Director of The Thomas Hardy Society).

There were six finalists with one winner, one runner up and four who were awarded Highly Commended Certificates.

The organiser, Rebecca Paveley from the National Trust, said: 'We hoped that the prize would inspire the young people of today living in the landscape which Hardy loved to try their hand at poetry. The competition showed us just how much talent, creativity and passion there is out there among young people.'

The winning entries for the inaugural National Trust Thomas Hardy Young Poetry Prize 2019 were celebrated with an awards afternoon at Hardy's home Max Gate.

As a result of the success of this year's competition, the National Trust has decided to run the competition annually and to extend it beyond Dorset so that entries may be submitted by any young poets anywhere. Entries for 2020 will be open from November.

Winner

National Trust Thomas Hardy Young Poetry Prize 2019

Reading 'A Wife in London'
Kitty Fisher – Year 9 at Colyton Grammar School

I read a Hardy poem once,
whilst chewing a Polo in class.
My teacher spoke of assonance
and how to grab the reader fast.

Every word, a shard of bone,
butchered and cold.
The way the poem loved to drone
made it tedious to be told.

Until I saw that dismantled skeleton rise,
each phrase, passionate like stars in Dorset's skies.
Tragedy was layered, tempting as fondant on a cake,
irony oozing from the centre, a sour gooseberry bake.

I adored every letter that surfaced as I read,
rhythmic and beautiful, like a sea inside my head.

The brutal tale that lashed like waves on rocks, ripped my feelings apart.
And now that monumental poem holds a grip upon my heart.

Thomas Hardy's poem was so dark, intense and utterly cruel.

Thomas Hardy's poem was the best thing I ever read at school.

Runner up

National Trust Thomas Hardy Young Poetry Prize 2019

The Wind Watches
Leonie Cobban – Year 9 at The Thomas Hardye School

From the lightest caress across the face
To the loud smack of the raging storm
The wind is ever present.
It is normality.

It carries the first fledglings of the spring as they flutter fleetingly
Towards able parents, the wind a caring guardian.
In Grandma's garden, the breeze brushes against her washing;
Green skirts, blue dresses, a spotty sock left by a forgetful grandchild.
Across the field, the new postman edges his way through the trees
Branches crackle under his feet and he feels the fresh breeze.
It is Spring. The wind lies quiet, tired after a long winter.

It lies waiting as the now-experienced fledglings soar
Up into the blue blanket above, their parents long gone.
At Grandma's house, the grandson wishes for a cool brush of wind
As he tosses grains of sand from one hand to the other, his spotty socks
now dirty.
The postman knocks on the door, holding his child by the hand,
Her blond puff of hair is like a Rice Krispie, the grandson thinks.
It is Summer. The wind rests until the days age.

cont ...

It whips through the ruffled feathers of the spar-rows as they carry twigs for their nest
Their labour building a sanctuary for the dark days of the winter.
In Grandma's living room, she watches as the wind undresses the trees on the field
The torn leaves of amber, brown and deep red cascade in a swirling storm of colour.
She cannot quite remember – what is the boy's name?
The grandson and the postman's daughter play at her feet.
The postman hears the gentle whistle of the gust and the crackle of dead branches under his feet.
As he ambles across the field.
It is Autumn. The wind wakes and resumes its battle against the sun.

It blows and distorts the naked trees as the birds sit in their nest
They protect their three little speckled orbs of life.
The postman hears the relentless howls in his ears
He wanders up to Grandma's house. But she is hand in hand with the dark.
She crumples like ruffled bedsheets in front of the two small friends
And she is found.
It is Winter. The wind acknowledges the loss and lies still for a minute.

A month later, the new fledglings fly as the funeral procession begins.
The children walk hand in hand.

Highly Commended Certificate

National Trust Thomas Hardy Young Poetry Prize 2019

A Walk in the Park
Eloise Cray – Year 9 at The Thomas Hardye School

As I am walking,
I see the brilliant blue sky looking down on me
As I am walking,
I hear the distant traffic leaving me in silence
As I am walking,
I smell the green grass silently swaying to every breath of the wind
As I am walking,
I feel the gentle heat of the sun warming up my skin
As I am walking,
I taste the fresh breeze flowing through my body
As I am walking, I am alone with nature.

Highly Commended Certificate

National Trust Thomas Hardy Young Poetry Prize 2019

I'm Just a Tree
Eve Gilmour – Year 9 at The Thomas Hardye School

I have sheltered people from the rain,
And withstood the force a hurricane
I have cradled children in my arms
To others I've caused serious harms
My skin's baby soft but in a jagged cage,
That's become cracked with growth and age
Do people even notice me?
No, they don't, for I'm just a tree.

My body has become a house,
For countless beetles and a woodlouse
Behind many individuals have hid,
In a game of Hide-and-Seek as a kid
When heartless winter comes back around,
I lay my cloak of leaves upon the ground
How can I make people see
How nurturing nature can sometimes be?

Despite my age I still stand,
Tall and proud, like a soldier, roots buried deep in the land
And if my species was to die today,
Mankind would just fade away
I've witnessed more than you can know
I've seen the seasons die, and watched flowers grow
But do people ever notice me?
No, they don't for I'm just a tree.

Highly Commended Certificate

National Trust Thomas Hardy Young Poetry Prize 2019

1 March 2018, 2:36pm
Alice Padgett – Year 12 at The Thomas Hardye School

Oh? So I see
So it's not just me
So it was never just you and I
I don't mind

I don't mind my fractured chest
Devotion laid to rest
I don't mind if you veer left
Cut right through my middle

Instead of questioning who and how
Now I stand up, clear and loud
Anonymous in an anxious crowd
Who cares if I let that get me down
I'm only 17.

A whole lifetime of love awaits
Spend time with friends, laugh, debate,
Perform, take passion in the things you have
For your family love you so much
And these things if you do not clutch

You'll lose them as quick as it begun

Highly Commended Certificate

National Trust Thomas Hardy Young Poetry Prize 2019

The Wind
Aiden Phillips – Year 9 at The Thomas Hardye School

The wind always breathing but never needs air,
Always watching with a cold icy stare.
The wind as sharp as a blade
That never needs sharpening.
The wind sees everything
But has no eyes,
The wind always following,
And never leaves someone behind.
The wind can hear everything,
And has no ears.
The wind will always be here,
And never ages.
The wind can be in the past,
But can also tell the future.

The Thomas Hardy Victorian Fair

Sunday 2 June 2019

I went to the fair
Lydia Martin – Aged 6 years

I went to the fair
and I had a pare
and I went up a stair
with a pare of shoes.

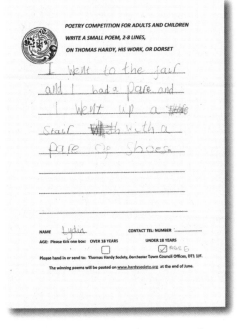

Amongst the many interesting events and displays during the Thomas Hardy Victorian Fair, children were invited to submit a few lines of poetry. They could write on any subject that they wished. This winner, Lydia Martin from the Bishop's Hull Primary School in Taunton, was awarded a copy of *Chosen Poem of Thomas Hardy* – selected and edited by James Gibson and published by The Thomas Hardy Society. In selecting this poem for a prize, one judge had this to say about Lydia's lines: 'I think that this is delightful. This young lady appears captivated by her shoes – new or acquired especially for the day? – the most important thought on her mind as she goes around the Fair. This unique effort deserves a book of *Chosen Poems*. In years to come this young poet will remember treading in the footsteps of Thomas Hardy at the Fair and how perhaps she first heard about him.'

A Poet's Thought
Thomas Hardy

It sprang up out of him in the dark,
And took on the lightness of a lark:
It went from his chamber along the city strand,
Lingered awhile, then leapt all over the land.

It came back maimed and mangled. And the poet
When he beheld his offspring did not know it:
Yea, verily, since its birth Time's tongue had tossed to him
Such travesties that his old thought was lost to him.

Seven students from Years 10 and 12, encouraged by Mr Nick Kelly, took part in the Thomas Hardy Poetry Workshop. They felt that the session inspired creativity and encouraged versification. They reported that they particularly enjoyed 'rewriting' Hardy which they felt allowed them to use his work as a writing scaffold to create new poems.

Iona's Heart
Ivor Davies

What childlike glee overcame me at the lowering of that barrier,
At the time no words could depict such purity,
No gleaming sun nor scorching rays compared to its dense
outstretched grass;
Nor tumbling waves or divine tastes match its wandering, glassy seas.
Its coarse, bouldered hilltops varnished with corals of rose blossoms,
    One jewel at the north of the isle: a lonesome, long abandoned
marble quarry.
It is different there, separate from time.
One everlasting, unceasing tide of serenity.

Although time has struck me, things that once provided equal bliss,
faded.
Lost from recollection, grey
Iona's heart remains constant, its romantic character unchanged;
Same sea-birds call caught in blistering ocean winds,
Now as that barrier lowers again, and as nostalgia proceeds to poke
at my smile
    Once again returned to that first time, Iona's heart embraces me.

After 'An August Midnight'
Serena Forwood

A ray of sun and the mutter of leaves
The mark of a minute, faster than it seems
On this scene enter – nerves, anticipation and dread –
Children, pupils, peers; all longing for bed.
Row upon row, behind and beside
Away from sun, trapped inside …

An Interlude
Eliza Harwood

A glowing lamp and an open blind,
and a chime of the abbey in a distance:
On this scene enter – joyous, bright and warm-hued
A caterpillar, a butterfly and a snail
Whilst consumed by thoughts
a hummingbird hums its song ...

Here our group gathers, in this cosy room
Stuck in time, whilst life carries on.
My movements disrupted, as my thoughts derail
the melody continuing on,
harmonies praising, celebrating,
growing louder and louder.

We the youth
Eliza Harwood

We the youth,
We the voice,
We the hope

We the truth,
We the noise,
We the soap,

We the new.
We the regretful.
We the ignorant.

We the relief,
We the belief,
We the sheaf,

We the you,
We the us,
We the tomorrow.

Locked, Unlocked
Nicole Liou

A dusty lamp and heavy blind,
And the memories from the distant past:
On this scene enter – trapped, panicked and fragmented –
A moment, a year and a lifetime;
While holding my wine there ripples spread
A sudden shiver, it reaches out its hand
Thus see us all, in that unfailing place,
That point of life, at that point in space.
The recollection faded my rationality,
And band on the lock for desires and fragility.
'God's the most compassionate, isn't he?' I muse. Yet why?
He knows my pain that know not I.

Cape Cornwall School
St Just – Cornwall
Headteacher: Sarah Crawley

A Young Man's Epigram on Existence
Thomas Hardy

A senseless school, where we must give
Our lives that we may learn to live!
A dolt is he who memorizes
Lessons that leave no time for prizes.

Ten students from Year 10, cheered on by Ms Kellie Rushberry, took part in the Thomas Hardy Poetry Workshop. They particularly enjoyed writing the group poems. They also reported back that the discussions were good – in particular, they felt confident to speak out and to respond as critical friends to what others had written. Many said that writing in imitation of Hardy's structure was exciting. Some students suggested that future similar sessions could include other nineteenth-century poets on themes similar to those of the Hardy poems selected.

The students concluded that reading and writing poems 'was fun'. Consequently, several chose to submit more than one poem. All poems submitted were included in this Anthology as promised in the initial briefing (see the Preface, Afterword and Appendix 2 for more details).

Collaborative Genius Interlude:

This poem was composed by all the students after
discussing Hardy's poem 'An August Midnight'.

An Impoverished Poet

An IKEA lamp and a cheapish blind,
And the silence of a clock from a dusty floor
When from the window they emerge – winged, horned, and spined.
A spider, a moth, and a bumblebee;
While amid the floor there shabbily lies that most hateful inventions for eyes to see,
All five of us meet in this lonely area
Amidst the passing, hate, love and naught of life,
These visitors rest on my tattered page
Or lay on my keyboard or eat off my uncleaned plates
'God's most insignificant creation.' I think, but why are they?
They know secrets of the world that I do not.

Exquisite Corpses Interlude:

All the students collaborated on writing this poem.

Being in Love

I woke up early today and laughed
The sun shone the fold of the curtain,
The refracted light glows an orange blaze through the room,
Casting a golden coat of light upon the footwork floorboards.
The door fell open, hinges yearning to be released.
No lament or fear fell about you, I took you once more
It really isn't like that anymore
When you walk in through the door
I am caught up in those starry eyes of yours.
All I felt was happiness and joy
An emotion I cannot tell overwhelmed me.

The naughty pony sonnet
Elsa Bowkett

Where has this led?
To my landing on my head,
When my pony bucked me off,
Right into a tree.
Next time my pony bucks me off,
I might go to the moon.
That's where I thought I might fly,
When my pony jumped too high.
Once he stood upon my foot,
And leaned on it so hard that he squashed my wellie boot.

Regret
Elsa Bowkett

Now I feel regret
To what this has led,
To my flying through the air, and landing on my head.
Yes, it hurt very much,
Landing on my head.

When this love backfired,
Quite literally,
For my pony bucked me off,
Right into a tree.
And right into a tree,
My pony bucked me off.

Another time,
My pony jumped so high,
I flew with him too,
It's a good thing that I stopped,
Or I might've gone to the moon.
Next time my pony bucks me off,
I might go to the moon.

As a parting farewell,
My pony stood upon my foot,
The throbbing in my right toe,
Will remind me where he put,
All of his weight.
Most people would turn to hate,
When all this has been done,
And turn and flee,
When their pony is naughty.

The Beach at Night
Dylan Cole

It is midnight and all is calm,
Waves lap against the shore, glowing gently by the moonlight,
Pebbles wash up and down with the sea foam,
The silk like soft sand falls with the wind,
A beam of bright light cascades from the hanging moon
Creating a line of white shimmering ripples going from far out
to sea back into shore, like a pathway to the horizon,
the light of a distant town's street-lights patching the sea
with a yellow glow.

Sitting not so far away
Dylan Cole

While we were sitting,
Sitting not so far away,
Remembering the games we used to play,
Recognising your voice through the noise,
While we were sitting,
Sitting not so far away.

While we were walking,
Still not so far away,
Hearing the sea and feeling the spray,
Nothing I could want more than being here and talking,
While we were walking,
Still not so far away.

I hear a sound come dancing,
Footsteps not so far away,
'Welly boots' trudging on the murky day,
The familiar sound bringing a memory prancing,
Footsteps not so far away.

Masses against the Classes
Morgan Denley

Deeper and deeper into the hole we go,
Clinging on for dear life but all help screams no,
We are the penniless and this is all we know.

Every day we fight for a living,
While the rich sit in their cushioned thrones singing,
Every day we fight to survive,
For we are the class that's been deprived
Of opportunities for life.

Growing up we are told that the sky is the limit,
But the only limit for us,
Is our social status.
Who wants to employ us?
For we are the 'filth' of your 'blessed society'
Therefore, we deserve to suffer!

But do we really need to suffer?
It's just your Wi-Fi won't stop its buffer
And get up to speed
And satisfy the need
And dig us out of our hole.

We're trapped and can't escape,
It's about time to change your social landscape
And realise everyone is the same,
We're not just a dog that's too hard to tame!

After We First Embraced
Morgan Denley

When we first embraced,
Things were much simpler,
We rushed through life,
Went from place to place,
After we first embraced,
Things were much simpler.

After we looked back,
Back on that which has come before,
We sparked into war,
Bombarded, I sat waiting for the next attack,
When we looked back,
Everything fell apart.

Now times have changed,
You're moving on,
But I have nothing to prolong my sorrow,
Nothing to con my sorrow to joy,
Now times have changed,
And I simply can't cope.

All was bliss and ignorance
Jago Dougan

All was bliss and ignorance, when I saw you this day.
The boy in me rushed back, alight with childhood glee.
All was bliss and ignorance, when I saw you this day.

We were jolly and joyful, no signs of dismay.
Our years were long and plentiful, my happiness remained outstanding.
We were jolly and joyful, no signs of dismay.

Like the maggot and the apple, our love would steadily decay.
You wouldn't see me at all, how our love took such a fall.
Like the maggot and the apple, our love would steadily decay.

We went on for years, perchance, till that day.
My resentment and anger, all overcome by sorrow.
All was bliss and ignorance, perchance, until that day.

Without
Jago Dougan

The sun rises, a vast curtain of light
The morning cold, chilling as ice.
The light vanquishing the remnants of night.

The light is warm, though I feel no heat.
The ice inside me burns hotter than any morning chill.
The shadow comforts me.

I can no longer remain, an insubstantial husk.
As I wake up, the fresh air drowns me.
For I cannot breathe, cannot love, cannot live

The ever advancing darkness threatens me.
So I let it, let the darkness possess me.
For what is the point of fighting.

Why do the birds keep on singing?
Why do the waves rush to shore?
Do they know or fathom my loss?

An eternity of existential awaits.
Because without you, I have no light, no love, no hope.

Rain
Vashti Foss

The crying sky rested upon my head.
Its tears came down upon my cheeks.
And behind those tears that I could see.
A hidden pain well-known to me.

Creatures
Vashti Foss

Hidden away from looking eyes
In a world well known to me
The creatures hide away in the dark
Afraid of what they'll see.
A world so full of hate and violence
They wouldn't last a day.
Be hunted down or captured and caged
So now they hide away.

Those few moments
Vashti Foss

As you grow up,
It all becomes forgotten.
Those few moments,
That time has turned to rotten.
Those times spent happy and free,
But that is now gone.
Those times spent laughing and dancing,
But time has passed on.
Don't let it happen to your own life,
Don't let those good few moments pass on by.

When I first met you
Vashti Foss

When I first met you,
I thought it would last forever,
But not even I could see the truth,
About how we couldn't stand being together.

When I first met you,
My heart was filled with happiness,
If only I knew then what I know now,
About how we would both feel sadness.

As time went by we grew apart,
And not even we could stand up and take the fault.

When I first met you,
I fell in love,
But we grew so far apart,
And now you are gone.

Closure
Millie Griffiths

The world keeps moving ever on,
Although I left its beaten track,
And find myself, alone at last,
Sitting in an empty field.

I look up. The sound of ravens;
Deathly black. Reverberates inside my head,
As wheeling they flock above me;
In the dusky skies.
But still the world moves ever on.

As night draws near, I rest my head.
My journey finally over.
And as my vision starts to fade, I understand;
The world moves ever on.

Conversations
Millie Griffiths

A man came up and spoke to me.
He spoke of times unknown.
He spoke of times forgotten.
He spoke of the white, and the black, and the grey,
But never once did he speak to me.

As I Sit underneath this Tree
Millie Griffiths

As I sit underneath this tree
A passer-by waves their hand, or nods their head,
And I reply: "Good day to you!"
And they continue on their way.

As I sit underneath this tree
A child calls out, or a cat meows,
And I am content,
As they continue on their way.

But as I sit underneath this tree
Not a soul walks past; all is silent.
The night is looming,
As I sit underneath this tree.

As I stand underneath this tree
I know it's time that I must go,
For there is no-one left to say "Hello"
Until I find some new tree, or park bench,
Where I can sit until day's end.

Whence First We Met
Millie Griffiths

Whence first we met,
A hundred miles from home,
I saw you standing alone,
Outside the churchyard.
When first we met
A hundred miles from home.

Whence first we met,
I should've known,
Love at first sight alone,
Is not enough.
Whence first we met
I should've known.

Whence first we met,
I should've said,
With a clear head;
"Let's wait a while."
Whence first we met
I should've said …

Opal Eyes
Lilly Robinson

Through opal eyes,
Attentively, I adore,
Laughing with Luminous Light
That rests, patiently,
upon our favourite views
a cherub child
with blissful chuckling eyes
and sunbeamed smiles
caresses my stiff resistant mind.
This substance, that all fails to capture,
Slips and slides avoiding
Distrusting fates curious clasp
Like rouge red jelly that a
Child slurps through its tooth fairy teeth.
I watch time's plod
And it glances back at
Me and Light.
We chuckle slightly as we
Remember what it is like to be young …

Upon the Time I Met You
Lilly Robinson

We were like the waves
My dear, first mingled in the ocean
Waves together, seen in salty spray,
But our time was shortened and paved
By the working of the waves.

Soon the firm rock crumbled
Our selfishness, the sea
carelessly tried to search, fumbled
For the unknown lock and key
And lost, the firm rock crumbled.

Our salient and serene
Water was disturbed
Rage, rage we force the waves
Upon the resigned beach
You drifted free from our sea.

Our cliffs corrosion coursed
Through my bleating blood
I, the lost unscathed lamb,
Saw, for once, what I'd done.

2020
William Tuckett

When I went out one day
A couple of miles away
When I looked across the way I had nothing to Say
I was then gone
But for what I long
Is a couple of miles a way

I set off then
I saw her again
So then I approach
We became close
It seemed to work
So I saw her again

It's completely ruined I knew
I messed it up and so did you
I was at home on my chair I was sat
I wish I did this I wish you did that
It's completely ruined I knew
I messed it up and so did you

world's worst poem
William Tuckett

I don't know what to write at this moment in time
I'm trying to think of words that rhyme
I think every day
Who made poems anyway
I don't know what words to put in
This poem might end up in the bin

The bin is where this belongs
Because it is so bad
If you think it's good then you are wrong
And that is very sad
My pen's running out of ink
So I better keep it short
Which is actually ok
Because I'm getting a bit bored

So thank you for listening from the beginning to the end
And I hope you enjoyed because I won't be doing this again

Change
Leah Turner

What's wrong with the world that we livin' in?
Always denying we don't need to change,
Only bothered about the money that we makin',
Coz these days we makin' money strange,
Let's ship 'em drugs so they can deal each other,
Let's give 'em guns watch 'em kill each other,
Getting youth in the gangs nobody seems to care,
And police killin' the blacks,
Just a few more off the welfare,
Our streets are filled with cracks,
And prison cells are filled to stacks.

When we first met
Leah Turner

When I set out to find my love,
A long journey away,
The sun glistening on the bay,
Could she be the angel from above?
When I set out to find my love,
A long journey away,

Where could she be? My love,
Up to heaven I stare,
Although I'm not aware she is there,
Falling gently the feather of a dove,
Where could she be? My love,
And still to heaven I stare,

When I had found my love,
I look into her eyes,
As heavenly as an evening sunrise,
My angel from above,
I had met my one and only love,
I look into her eyes.

Careless World
Alex Way

I will make a world,
Boundless, Magnificent, Divine,
Filled with lands,
Mountains, Hills, Plains,
Give it a sea,
Bays, Atolls, Rivers,
Animals that live amongst that divine,
Beings who think, Create, Discover,
They make things, Great inventions, A step forwards,
They pick from the ripe, Entrusting branch,
Within soil, Within earth, On land and sea,
But they're doing it wrong,
They hunt wrongfully, for trophy and bragger,
They kill needlessly, to satisfy the powerful,
But most of all,
The world I made for them,
It's dying, they're killing it,
It's sad to see the young, the powerless, ask for a change,
But the leaders? They don't listen,
They feed, They harvest, Bite and bite away,
Soon to be world, Dead and still,
Dying and dying, Beyond mortal repair,
To what ends did I summon this divine earth?
The once prosperous land I saw before me,
Is but a barren wasteland,

The wind had blown,
But not anymore.

In 2020
Alex Way

When I had first met you,
We were struck by our gaze,
First sight we knew, love was no haze,
We were friends at first, talked where, what and who,
Before our hearts had formed into two,
Looking back now, this was all just a phase,

After I had first met you,
Any tell we had yield,
We frolicked through field,
Last year where I had found you,
To propose, to confess, I kneeled,

In 2020, all said and done,
I no longer yearn, for your grace or touch,
Grow apart you said, think I not much,
In 2020, where our hearts had spun,
Now wither and wilt, not woven to bun,

In 2020, I now know you not,
My heart is lost, gone far away,

Dorchester Middle School
Dorchester – Dorset
Headteacher: Caroline Dearden

The High-School Lawn
Thomas Hardy

Blades of Grass
Dorchester Middle Students

Gray prinked with rose,
White tipped with blue,
Shoes with gay hose,
Sleeves of chrome hue,
Fluffed frills of white,
Dark bordered light;
Such shimmerings through
Trees of emerald green are eyed
This afternoon, from the road outside.

Everything stops.
When it's cut.
Morning Dew.
Green knees.
Bugs crawling around.
Flowers blooming across the field.
Waving in the breeze.
Dig your hand into the grass.
You forget the number you're on.

They whirl around:
Many laughters run
With a cascade's sound;
Then a mere one.

A bell: they flee:
Silence then: –
So it will be
Some day again
With them, – with me.

Twelve Year 8 students, supported by Mr Rob Murray, took part in the Workshop. They felt that the session inspired creativity. They reported that they particularly enjoyed 'rewriting' Hardy, which they felt allowed them to use his work as a writing scaffold to create new poems. A walk on the school lawn included a description of how, as a mathematics project, the students counted the blades of grass. This, in turn, produced the poem above. The students' evaluation of the session was entirely positive.

Out
Anonymous

A strange feeling,
They feel themselves going away
As if their skin were peeling
Every day.

People want it to be false
People want it to fade
And as I hear my singing pulse
They crawl into the shade.

But what is it,
a trait of mine,
who shares it,
and why is the world blind?

Why is it hated and loved,
a sign of religion and nihilism,
and why do only some possess it,
some say disease,
others say choice,
also something only carriers of the trait can voice.

When you grow up in a world, secure and safe,
for you to be banished back in
when you'd rather be out.

You can be lucky, rich or smart
for it doesn't change you academically,
only when you voice do some cringe.

Feeling loved is something everyone desires,
So why do some extinguish others' fires?
I could only dream of such spite, because
where I live agree it's alright.

Night
Poppy Bessant

The gentle breeze calls me,
I close my eyes.
Birds sing,
Bees buzz,
I hum.
The sun beats down on me,
warmth prickles my skin.
I can hear the quiet rustling of the branches,
The gentle echo of footsteps.
I smile,
at one with the world.

Breathe Out
Josh Bray

The concrete clicks below my feet,
an unnamed bug flies just as I feel the wind;
a light breeze rolling over my face.
The world tranquil, as if this place
populated once with life and death,
deserted now, it's find breath.
breathe in.

The leaves crackle and crunch
Below my step, there isn't much left here.
The roaring machine of change whirls past,
an empire falls, built over, we never asked for this.
So why?
Breathe out.

Again.
Faster now, my heart racy,
my breaths echo through the ages.
Screams prevail in their onslaught through time.
Breathe in.

Everything Stops
Mischa Dearden

Elongated roots swim through the undergrowth,
Blue-birds whisper lullabies in my ear
Everything stops.

I stroll across the blazes of grass
Daffodils blooming,
A drop of water touches the morning dew
Everything stops.

A breeze of guilt dances past me
The devil touches my skin
I drown myself in sorrow
Everything stops.

* * * * *

<u>Poet's notes:</u>

Elongated roots swim through the undergrowth.
Everything stops.
I stand there watching.
Blue birds whisper lullabies in my ear.
Morning dew.
Light breeze.
I stroll across the morning dew like a lone cloud.

Still out of Sight

Persis Ebenezer

It sits there … always.
Quiet and awake,
gasping for breath, trying to live.
Wishing to be taken in by the light
But it seems to be far, far still out of sight.

Invisible
Rosie-Drew Howard

Do you see them?
Of course not, no one can.
Hidden in plain sight, right in front of your eyes.

They think like you, talk like you,
Even look like you.
But what makes them different isn't
Skin deep, it's in your control.

You did that,
You made it so no one could hear
Them, no matter how loudly they shouted.
They could do the silliest dance routine and still no one would see.

But why won't you listen? Take notice?
Give them a minute, see what once couldn't be seen.
See what had been invisible, hear what hadn't been heard,
Take not eyes off something has previously
Been ignored, view them with new eyes.

But you won't.
Because everyone would rather they
Stayed invisible while you shined bright
As a star, stood out against the night sky.

When will things change?
When will the unseen be seen?
I don't know. That's up to you.

Free
Jemima Larkin

ruffling feathers,
wings reach out,
a tingle inside you,
you're ready to go.

all of a sudden,
you're up in the air,
gracefully gliding,
touching the sky.

feeling the clouds,
breathing it in,
the breeze and the freshness.

Finally free.

Walking Away
Sophia Liddicott

It's hard to do it
It always has been
And always will be

Walking away from happiness
From sadness a fight a song
We enjoy to let a moment linger
But as soon as it's there
It will be gone

We want to be the last one standing
To be seen most powerful
We want to be seen as a brave person
To be the last one out of danger

But sometimes it's best to walk
Step by step.

Just Wondering
Sophia Liddicott

What are you doing
Just wondering
So am I
About my life good looking
The guys
The essays
The punishments
What I'm doing next
What about you
Why should I open the window and see
The world?

The Clouds Were Breached
Emma Locke

The clouds were breached,
in the open sky,
failing to cover their tracks,
for all angels' flight has broken them,
in a methodical attack.

The breeze was brisk,
in the open field,
in a warming of winter's bite,
for an angels' wings have broken the peace,
expending their beautiful might.

The sun filtered through the branches,
onto the open ground,
but still the ground was cold,
for an angel's grief has frozen the land,
keeping it from the devil's hold.

Yet still,
I sit by the side of the angels,
their wings left in the sky,
for they have saved me,
forevermore,
and taught me how to fly.

Although their halos broken,
and feathers of pure white gone,
these angels have brought forth happiness to me,
as though I heard their song.

Baldness
Kitty McFarland

Baldness it's a funny thing really
You touch your head
Nothing
You scratch your head
Nothing
You wash your head
Nothing

New Life
Kitty McFarland

Seeing new life is a pleasure
Its big gangly legs
Struggling to stand but trying to run
Learning to balance its weight
Falling flat on its face
Watching new life is a pleasure

Journey
Oisín Murphy

Where am I going
I pass the halls of joy
Outline the features of a smile
I carry on

When will I stop
I enter a café of people
So many yet no two
I carry on

Who will help me
I open the door to burning
The heat clawing at my skin
I carry on

What am I doing
I interrupt a room sorrow
I am infused with guilt of actions
I carry on

Why am I doing this
I join in groups of bonds
The bonds form steadily yet break easily
I carry on

I stop
I pause
I fall

This is new

Stages of a Poem
Cameron Webb

Heat of the sun
Shadow of the clouds
Constant chirp of the crickets,
Occasional shouts and splashes
Grass, bone dry
But filled with life
Marching ants
Bees, buzzing, looking for something sweet
Planes, leaving criss-crossing streaks
Rustle of the trees
Smell of pollen

Heat of the sun
Shadow of the clouds
Rustling trees
Grass, bone dry
But filled with life
Chirping crickets.
Marching ants.
Bees, buzzing.
Looking for something sweet.
Shouts, splashes,
Bikes, squeaking brakes.

Heat of the sun
Shadow of the clouds
Rustling trees
Grass, bone dry,
But filled with life
Chirping crickets
Marching ants
Bees buzzing,
Looking for something sweet
Shouts, Splashes,
Bikes, Squeaking brakes.

Greenwood Academy
Birmingham
Headteacher: Allen Bird

The Caged Goldfinch
Thomas Hardy

Within a churchyard, on a recent grave,
    I saw a little cage
That jailed a goldfinch. All was silence save
    Its hops from stage to stage.

There was inquiry in its wistful eye,
    And once it tried to sing;
Of him or her who placed it there, and why,
    No one knew anything.

From 'Caged'
Jessica-Jayne Lucas

We meet in the room anger in his eyes
The bitterness of air and in atmosphere despise.
At this point in time, at this point in space.
I was wondering how I can ever escape.
My guts disperse as tears roll down my face
Please – no not in this space –
Not in this time or place of year.
Please not let one more tear …

Fifteen Year 10 students, emboldened by Ms Charlotte Hammond, took part in the Thomas Hardy Poetry Workshop. They reported that poetry allowed them 'to say what you couldn't say elsewhere …'. One student said: 'I've never been a great fan of poetry. Now, I feel that I have become a poet ….' His participation was enthusiastic and his poem was deeply evocative. Students also reported that the teacher was very passionate about poetry which made the session really exciting. They agreed that 'today's sad and challenging world needed poetry to alleviate its misery'.

53

Polluted memories ...
Lewis Carr

Here lies the ancient grounds of my old happiness,
Polluted, decayed and empty,
Here was the entrance
Where my mind once wandered off.

She stood there staring into the distance
proud of what she had created;
The boy who ran around, screaming with laughter,
Had forgotten the lost memories of his "father".

Like a frantic puppy, he ran further into the distance.
Danger, fear and corruption did not
Occur to him, but the ball of happiness stood
watching the boy – still proud of what she created fifteen years later.

My Childhood
Ana Cristea

Once upon a time,
When the day was longer,
And the night was shorter,
When the kids were brighter,
And the memories were better.

Childlike me, was dancing in the sea,
And the wind was leaning to see,
What's next going to be.

The fire was brighter than bright,
And I was happier than the light,
All of a sudden I sit down to see,
A creature looking at me ...

The ancient floor
Chanel Hill

Here is the ancient floor,
To the side of the walls, the wooden cupboards adorned
Here was the former door,
To which the injured woman stumbled in, hospital gown still worn

She stood there, smiling widely in the door frame,
As she bent down, slowly, picking things up in pain
Although she was probably mad that I made a mess of her kitchen
I know she was glad to finally be with me

After weeks of medicine and endless treatment
I was glad that she was finally capable of leaving
I knew she wouldn't be able to do everyday things
Like taking me to the park and pushing me high on the swings

Using her hands, arm and leg may bring her some issues
But let's not be sad, let us be grateful. Put away the tissues!
She will soon go into surgery again after about 10 years
I will be strong though, just like you grandma, I will hold back my tears!

Memorial Memory
Alastair Hill-Weddle

Upon that high hill top, pointing like a knife
The spire of Thiepval stood, towering over all forms of life
The shape of it, like stairs
My smile fails to tears
Oh how could such magnificence and awe
Come from such hell as war?
I tore up those steps, white with purity
And the names it contains are plenty.
Half British, Half French, all courageous
Lists upon lists, I scanned for that one man
"I hope I can find him" I thought, "Yes I can!"
T'was near the bottom his name, a name in memory I can add
Henry Milburn Weddle, my Great-Great Grandad.
His role in the Army of the King, Company Quartermaster Sergeant
I know that is a role where you have to be urgent.
I read on, found the First Day of the Somme, the day he died on,
Yet he means so much to me,
Now forever in my family tree,
This imperative day never shall leave me.

El Flores[1]
Jessica-Jayne Lucas

Walking around a crowded market,
Wondering where my Grandad had parked it;
The car.
The wind whispered in my ear,
As I heard the others cheer.

Strolling around my hand in my Grandma's,
Thinking we lost Grandad, but he wasn't too far.
Jumping out and scaring me,
There stood my grandad as careless as can be.
Me as little and innocent as ever,
I ran over to the flowers not knowing any better.

Can I get some for mum I asked,
As very little time went past.
I reached into my pocket to get the last.

In the end it was all worth it,
Now I look back it was so perfect.

Gift giving is loving and caring,
Everyone needs to learn the necessity of sharing.

---

1   The flowers (Spanish).

Memories

Jessica-Jayne Lucas

There lies the newly laid floor,
I once walked upon before.
Happy memories I think not,
The last of those were in the cot.
I once stood where many had stood before,
Laughing, crying emotions all raw.

She lay there in that bed,
And I was overcome with a sense of dread.
I stood there still, not knowing what to do.
While everyone around was full of blue.

Doctors rushed in, full of panic,
While my head was full of manic.
All of those emotions, I felt then,
I kept them all in my den.

Seven years on and still not great,
Though we mustn't mess with fate.
There is a plan for us all after all,
We just need to go along for the ball.

Barbie House
Alicia Madaleno

There she is,
Sitting near the door,
With no sis
On her bedroom floor.

With her legs crossed
Talking to her Barbie
She was never lost
Who she named Marlie

Maybe lost in her imagination,
She was once a child,
Her Barbie house was her admiration
With dreams running wild.

She was fed up,
Some called her weird, some called her crazy,
She did not want to grow up
But she couldn't help not to like the smell of a daisy!

Childlike Achievements
Phoebe McFarlane

The journey seemed to last forever,
As we drove over the bridge and across the river;
Cobbled, curved and uneven,
I wait impatiently to reach our destination.
I finally convinced my family to get a dog,
Begging them as we drove through the fog.

Childlike, I celebrated at my achievement,
As I reached the door with defiance,
And searched desperately for the one;
The one who I would call mine;
And I would care for like a child,
Even though I was a child.

The Beach
Charlotte Parkes

The hands on the clock mean as much as dirt,
Worries wither away like flowers in winter.
The rays bleach my hair and redden my skin,
My heart, my soul, my hope couldn't catch a splinter.

The water heats and smiles brighten,
Beaming sun from a bright diamond sky.
Wet clothes and salt, ocean washed and painted,
I met my family's content, hopeful eyes.

Sand gathers in the creases of denim shorts,
Care for this is long and far gone.
Even the shade means to be kind to us,
Worries, doubt, fears, when counted are none.

The figure outside
Ida Samba

She was sitting
On the floor gazing
at the window, smiling
as the trees dance and sway

Something catches her eye.
A man? A woman? A child?
She could not say.

She tells herself
Not to worry and
Closes the blinds
In a hurry

Her curiosity builds.
She opens the blinds.
Darkness. Not a speck of light the figure nowhere in sight.

She wonders what it was she saw
as she turns around but she did not finish that thought.
She was never seen again.

Untitled Poem
Molly Selby

There I laid, as the trees swayed
And I just prayed, wished even
That this day wouldn't end

And there she was,
A tear in her eye
And a beer in her hand
As she watched the bright golden sun
Descend into the white nefarious clouds of the unknown

Trampoline
Romany Taylor-Bartlett

Here lies the springy trampoline,
Shiny and silver and thick,
Here was the big one
Who made that day great

He jumped and jumped,
Laughing and laughing,
As he knocked me off
The shiny and silver trampoline

Me as a child laughed,
As well until I felt the
pain, the pain in my arm
More and more each time

Three
Wajia Timar

There I laid low in what felt like a fluffy cloud,
My eyes flickered like a lamp,
As I struggled to open my eyes.
My petite hands rubbed against my sore eyes
Finally my eyes struck open as I felt a presence
near me. As my eyes focus on a figure who was
A devil in disguise. His sneer grew bigger as he walked
in tune as his heels clicked like the broken clock which
lay lifelessly above me. His devilish eyes fixed into my
angelic eyes made me tear with fright. At the age of three I felt
Like I had seen the devil itself.

My body stone cold as the malevolent figure grabbed me and
clutched me in his arms. I wailed painfully as I felt like pressure
hitting my ribs from him like he was wanting to kill me, his
powerful force controlled me like I was a peasant and he was
the king. What did he want from me?

One Spring Day
Bethany Tracey

My feet pattered relentlessly against the steel floor,
As my mother cooked a meal.
Her long, auburn hair cascading down her back,
Her skills lack.

But I am comforted by her warm embrace,
Her bright, shining smile as she stores leftovers in case.
The chuckles of my brother chime,
As he pretends to be a mime.

Now my happiness is soaring,
As I listen to my dog's roaring.
Will ebullience come my way?
Or will my hidden anger stay?

La Playa[2]
Abigail-Naomi Turnbull

One summer afternoon,
At the beach the gentle wind blowing through my hair,
The bright blue sea stood rolling in front of me,
The golden sun kissed sand stood still.

Mis primos[3] were dancing and splashing in the sea;
My mother stood observing with a watchful eye,
My sister seemed half asleep on the sand,
Curled in a ball under the tree so tall.

Dancing in the sunlight,
Thankful for such a wonderful day;
Everything was perfect;
Including my dad and me.

---

2   The beach (Spanish).
3   My cousins (Spanish).

A Trip to Your Imagination
Charlie Wattis

Here it is,
A building of dreams,
where your imaginary thoughts flow like streams.
Glowing and spectacular,
My eyes widened as I entered.
I'm in a dark room,
And a flash of the giant screen blinds my eyes.

My eyes start to adjust,
As I witness a world of your imagination.
My mind is blown.
My mind is speaking to me,
Screaming all these feelings:
Sadness, Happiness, Excitement, Surprise.
The lights go out as I sit there thinking,
This Is My Future.

St Ives School
St Ives – Cornwall
Headteacher: Jan Woodhouse

The Sun on the Bookcase
Thomas Hardy

Once more the cauldron of the sun
Smears the bookcase with winy red,
And here my page is, and there my bed,
And the apple-tree shadows travel along.
Soon their intangible track will be run,
And dusk grow strong
And they have fled.

Yes: now the boiling ball is gone,
And I have wasted another day …
But wasted – *wasted*, do I say?
Is it a waste to have imaged one
Beyond the hills there, who, anon,
My great deeds done,
Will be mine always?

Eleven Year 10 students, encouraged by Mr Jonathan Hall, took part in this Workshop. They reported that they enjoyed collaborating on the group poem 'An August Midnight'. They found sharing Hardy's poems 'real fun' and were excited by the prospect of 'changing an old classic' like 'A Church Romance'. This session was noticeable for joviality and a great deal of laughter – especially when rewriting Hardy.

71

Collaborative Genius Interlude:

This poem was composed by the students after discussing Hardy's poem.

'An August Midnight'

A dirty lamp and tattered blind,
A broken chime from a distant ground,
Patterned, spiked, winged – entered the scene
A bumblebee, a caterpillar and a ladybird.
While within my dark works they shine innocent,
Insignificant, slumped there without sense,
As time slows, I sit in the company of my neighbours,
During the span, as I forget my labours,
One line broken, one sound misheard
Or shelter under the lamp, ambivalent yet assertive
'Lucky are they, in their oblivion' and yet
Our ignorance seems to be set.

Exquisite Corpses Interlude:

Students collaborated on writing this poem.

I watched hard and thought I saw

I watched hard and thought I saw
A shaded figure, bearing tooth and claw
The absence of feeling left
Sucked into a black hole, left bereft.
Awoke in perplexity
Asleep, yet very much awake
My shoulders in attempt of galvanising me, my mum did shake.
Awakening, my vision is slow, the sound of day returns
To my ear belonging, borrowed by the slumber that engulfs us.
But then that sound disappears into the mist without us,
The song has gone, it shall sing no more, I'm left alone, me and
my thoughts, yet the cacophony of silence is deafening,
Deafening to the point at which all sanity and relatively normal
thought completely disappear
I am broken. I have no thoughts, no cares
The world floats by, my thoughts are theirs.

The Laws of Nature
Felix Barker and Zac Chaney

He ambles with great intent, a burden on his shoulders
His laborious strut, with the speed of six legs, hastily he heads homewards.
The household of family, the network of love, is on the forefront of his being
In the distance appears his only want, his family he is seeing
One lunging assault, he is no more.

The stooping culprit, stride unbroken, flies away
The knight of death soon replaced by the light of day.
Her usual birds-eye view proves useless amongst this capping canopy
She lowers herself in hope to provide for her hopeless family.
As she glides down, her murderer pounces from the shadows.

Lurking on the scene, there is a mastermind at work
His feline-esque agility allows him to attack with a jerk
Without a further glance, yet at every moment seeing, he begins his roaming
Unknowingly, towards his fate like a missile he is homing
The grinding gears of the end of the line abruptly engulf him

Through this turn of events the mechanical menace proves to be the master
Mother is always maintaining life but man can destroy it faster.

Destruction
Ruby Barker

I spent my hours in a cloud today,
Yesterday, I floated in the ocean.
Last month, I skipped over hot burning sand,
And climbed a mountain with devotion.

As a child I ran through golden meadows,
Along the winding lanes,
I clambered over spring moorland:
I enjoyed my planet without pain.

But you have destroyed that.
And it won't be coming back.

1–10
Chloe Bryan

One thought, One mind
Two friends, Too kind
Three weeks, Three cries
Four walls, Four times
Five years, Five lies
Six lessons, Six professions
Seven days, Seven nights
Eight jokes, Eight fights
Nine tests, Nine bests

Eighteen years of hard work just to count to 10.

Divide
Toby Davies

A faint voice lies on the wind
A bellow once, yet now a whisper,
Words that soon will say they missed her
You'll all regret, but soon forget,
When life no longer lets you kiss her.

I shout so loud yet I'm not heard,
You look to me as if I'm absurd,
Madness must end before it's too late,
Before we reach that dreaded date.

We're going down, we're over the sea,
Two parachutes left, one for you, one for me,
Hear my voice, now or never,
Maybe you'll keep listening forever,
Hear my voice, now or never,
Maybe you'll keep listening forever.

We've run	out of luck
And run	out of Chance
We've got	to make a stand
To stop	is the only way
Before you leave	to the land above

The Tea Phenomenon
Lucas Hill-Whitthall

The plane of existence is not set in stone
The emergence of life can neither be denied nor admitted
That which we wish to obtain can often be as distant as a
burning star in the blackened sky
We live as we die

Suddenly

The apes laugh and prance at the thought of meaningless life
Behind the masks, fear eats at the soul
Such is the fate of all things, be they as different as a plank or
a pole
But many things aren't for us to decide
Even in death, there are laws we must abide.

Romancing In Church
Scarlett McMahon

The church bells started to ring,
The angel's strings began to sing,
When she gracefully walks:
There will be no more talks.
Its sweet aroma fills the air with its smell
Every soul in the church could tell –
That they, were in love.
'Thus their hearts' bond began, in due time signed'
Their love legally binds.
Today's bliss has brought joy,
Which said 'I claim thee as my own forthright'.

The Tea through the Window
James Morton

The liquid was poured from the pot,
It cascades down the milky china a drip
Is spilled over the side
And met with a face of disgust and dismay,

Out the window they do look, our eyes meet
I stare a while but admit defeat,
I stare again but realize the truth,
I can fly and fly and fly, fly, fly, fly, fly;

The creature flies and hits the glass
Sliding down it spasms, then does pass,
The man does stare again his creation lays, alas

The pot sits empty, empty as his heart.

The man sits down again, again,
Trapped in his box although he does cope

At least the creature,
Did have hope.

Why does the wall have so many pictures?
Nell Nankervis

Spending time alone with an absence of feeling,
The ceiling becomes of which a blanket.
Stares not welcome,
Judgement heard only from within.
There's a point where the numbness becomes ache,
That has to be released from the skin.

Smooth turns to broken. Open wound.
No one will know, it's hidden- consumed.
Just for a minute, emotion is present.
Just only an adolescent. Ignorant.

Solitary to the point no one is there to care,
There to look, imagine a life that is incomprehensible.
The wall has become a life I don't deserve,
Preserved by thoughts that are a lie.

Thank you pictures,
Now I know I have made no damage,
Hurt no one.
Leaving won't be a struggle.

The Weight of a World
Erin Veal

When an old door creaks, and a breeze fills the room,
Dismiss it, ignore it
For it does not foreshadow doom.

Do not let the mind wonder,
Do not lead the imagination astray,
For when you suspect the unexplainable,
Sanity starts to decay.

The creaks become screams,
Of origins which unknown.
The breeze becomes whispers,
Drenching to the bone.

Paranoia.

Left, right, all around
Fears follow everywhere
Flinch, turn, for there was a sound
Something wicked this way comes.

Melancholy found, send shivers through one's frame
Ancient myths of young yet old turn prayers to the soul
Silent cries of lust for sanctuary; don't trust, don't trust
Voices, voices, voices – people in my head
For death, for greed, for anger
Why not for peace?
It's so foggy I cannot see
Hell lives within me.

In Praise of Bad English
Heather Wilson

'You know your a writer if you just flinched'
Humanity's obsession with perfection is utterly obscure
Why must this matter so much when any communication is
just as pure,
I don't need to be told every single day,
That I'm unable to write the correct thing,
In the correct way.

School
Liv Yabsley

Albert Einstein once said, 'Everyone is a genius.
But if you judge a fish
On its ability to climb a tree,
It will live its whole life believing it is stupid'.

Day in, day out
Sat within these four walls
Raise my hand when I want to speak
Followed by a short break to eat
And for the rest of the day they
Tell me what to think.

I want to live in a world where what I think means something

In a world where school focuses on collaboration not competition

A world where individuality is celebrated not suppressed

A world where I'm not forced to be the same as
My peers – like a clone in a cruel system

Where some excel and others fall behind

In a world where fish are no longer forced to climb trees.

St Osmund's
Church of England Middle School
Dorchester – Dorset
Headteacher: Saira Sawtell

Waiting Both
Thomas Hardy

A star looks down at me,
And says: 'Here I and you,
Stand, each in our degree:
What do you mean to do, –
Mean to do?'

I say: 'For all I know,
Wait, and let Time go by,
Till my change come, – 'Just so,'
The star says: 'So mean I: –
So mean I.'

Fourteen Year 8 students, supported by Ms Anya February-Perring, took part in the Thomas Hardy Poetry Workshop. They enjoyed what they called the 'freedom to create'. They said they felt that Hardy's poems gave them ideas on what to write. They reported that they particularly liked the idea that when discussing poems read – including their own – there were no 'right or wrong' answers as long as the respondent gave reasons for his/her views with support from the text.

Exquisite Corpses:

Students collaborated on composing the following poem.

I woke early this morning

I woke early this morning.
Seasons are bright and colourful
Forever changing weather.
The seasons come and go as they please
Bringing bursts of everything new
Nothing else could compare
Or even dare
To take the risk.
And try to claim the reward.
But to seek the treasure
The treasure inside and out.
So amazing, what's it about
Everything around us, moving around
Listening to nature's sounds
Ignoring the cries of a devilish hound.

Silence Is the Answer and Nameless Is the Price
Anonymous

"Hello?" the girl cries, "is anybody there?
Will anyone throw me a hope or a care?"
"I am here." A voice rings out,
"I can help you without a shadow of doubt."

Hopeless and scared, the girl begged the voice,
But another said,
"You better think twice, because silence is the answer and
nameless is the price."

The girl agreed with the first voice within a heartbeat,
But the second voice persisted,
"Think about this carefully, because your choice will be obsolete."

"They're right you know," the first voice said,
"It will be obsolete, but then again, isn't it your life to complete."
"Don't listen to it!" the second voice cried.
"It is your choice, but don't listen to his lies!"

"He'll give you an offer and leave you in debt!
And what you owe him he'll never forget,
You'll agree once, twice then more.
Then what will you not depend on him for?"

"It's your choice girl, do the right thing,
Be smart about this don't accept the ring!"
"She has no choice!" the first voice snapped.
"She must depend on a husband and that is that!"
"Do not listen!" the second voice replied.
"You are your father's property, stay here by my side!"

cont ...

"But I don't need either of you," the young girl realised.
"I can be free, like a bird in the skies."
And with these words she pushed away the ring,
The voices stopped and faded away to nothing.

With no regret in her actions,
She then took flight,
Now a free bird,
Flying through the night.

The Sirens
Anonymous

Walking one day I hear the sirens blare,
I see them racing down to the city square.
On the news I later see,
A man was arrested, they say he murdered three.

Some do not know,
Most do not care.
They're more worried about their clothes or their hair.
They're too busy to realise what happened in the square.

Walking one day I hear the sirens screech,
I see them racing down towards the beach.
The news then reports the death of a woman so fair,
But once again, most do not care.

"It matters not," These people do say,
"Hundreds more die every day."
They then turn away and continue faking grief,
They pass the deaths by like an insignificant leaf.

They perform for the cameras,
Act all teary and sad,
Does anyone care?
Only time will tell.

When their actions summon them to heaven,
Or to hell.

There Is Not Much That I Can Do
Anonymous

There is not much that I can do
With my ideas, so few
In a world where I am insignificant
All I seem to do is rant.

But still, is there hope?
Or am I just on a downward slope?
Could a person change their fate?
Or is it just too late?

I will make a change,
My words will not derange,
I can make a difference,
I will make the world see sense.

What They Say
Joe Arthy

I step out into the starry night sky,
I see the Plough, Orion and the moon.
Space fascinates me and I don't know why,
I hope I can go there soon.

I imagine sailing in a sea so bright,
I think of planets and the milky-way,
I see darkness surrounded by tiny white lights,
And hear them talking, this is what they say.

They say, "Look at that marble, all green white and blue,
The inhabitants call it earth.
They live there and they kill it they do,
But they have no idea what it's worth."

I say, "Let's stop pollution,
Switch to nuclear and electricity.
We need a quick solution,
To make it the best earth it could be".

Comparing
Tamsin Burt[1]

We have the machines,
but does it suit our needs,
we have the cures,
but they needed it more,
we don't have the freedom
and we don't need them,
the money we needed,
we deserve it, we pleaded

We have to deal with pollution,
We need a solution,
Nature is dying,
No one should be smiling,
We just wanted to read and write,
To give us a chance to see the light,
We should be able to have a vote
I want to speak the words I wrote.

---

1 Tamsin Burt and Lucia Donkin-Turnbull (see next page) discussed their ideas, collaborated on a few lines and then individually wrote their separate poems which shared some lines.

We All Have Problems …
Lucia Donkin-Turnbull

Every world has problems …

We have the machines,
But does it suit our needs?
We have the cures,
But they needed it more.

They don't have the freedom,
And they don't need men.
The money they needed,
We earned it, they pleaded.

We have to deal with pollution,
We need a solution.
Nature is dying,
No one should be smiling.

They just wanted to read and write,
To give them a chance to see the light.
They should have had a vote,
They wanted to speak the words they wrote.

The world needs to solve them,
No one rules us, even the men.
We deserve the right pay,
Not just Teresa May.

The Zoggledeezee
Aneurin (Nye) James

Like a bird on a branch with its song in the wind,
I can hear its calling, what song did it sing?
I can hear its movements, the twitch in the tree,
The solemnly song of the Zoggledeezee.

I can hear it calling in the lonely night,
Looking for someone that it can soon take flight ... with
And my ears shudder in the breeze, of the song of that bird
that I cannot see.

The time is now morning, I hear no more song,
I give up my hope, my hope is now gone.
But I hear vibrations, I hear a pair,
I hear the not so lonely song of the bird that's there.

I can hear it calling in its summer flight,
Looking for food before the start of the night.
And my ears shudder in the gentle breeze,
Of the harmonic tune of the Zoggledeezee.

Everyone Dies One Day
Joe Kinsey

Everyone dies one day,
But your actions are left to stay,
From war to protests,
Actions speak louder than words. Nevertheless,
On the other hand,
Words also don't die,
And words empower actions,
Prophets and Authors use words with great meaning,
They inspire others to start protesting.

End of the Storm
Isla Menary

Silver droplets forming in the cotton puffs above,
Falling as they grow,
Falling to the ground.
Gently pattering, causing minute splashes.
Studding everything in a sparkling sheet of diamonds,
Crystalizing in the crisp winter air.
Rippling the water in an artistic display,
And decorating spider's webs,
As they rush out of the way.

Rapid clear bullets, overflowing the rivers,
Flooding the roads.
Working as an evil duo with the wind,
Hammering against the windows, desperate to enter.
Blowing the trees and knocking over the fences,
The trees creak and groan as they surrender.
The sky is ghostly grey now, casting shadow over the land,
Birds shriek and twitter frantically as delicate homes are destroyed.

But the storm has ceased now, the wind is dying,
The world is slowly creeping back to life.
Flowers sprout from the sodden ground,
Colours bursting like fireworks.
The ponds and lakes lie still as a mirror,
Reflecting the shining, bright ball of light,
Appearing through the departing clouds.
Spring has arrived.

A Painting Is a Story
Leila Phillips

A painting is a story.

However bold, however blue,
However big, however small,
However deep, however subtle,
Make it unique to you.

Fill it with joy, fill it with sorrow,
Fill the whole canvas, only fill the middle,
Fill it with colour, fill it with shades,
But don't let the story drain away.

Let it touch a heart, let it educate a brain,
Let it share an experience, let it play a game,
Let it inspire a child, let it trigger an idea,
Make something new appear.

Make a person smile, make them cry,
Make him laugh or make her hurt inside,
I'll make you rethink, make you imagine,
But always keep your story alive.

The Scrapbook's Journey
Leila Phillips

Water is a scrapbook,
Everywhere it goes it is imprinted with something new,
A splatter of colour, a dainty flower, a plastic cup,
The choice is up to you.

Each sea is a new page,
Adding something unique to the book,
Whether photo, poem or prose,
It's about the journey, take a look.

Recording emotions as the water flows from North, to South, to
East, to West,
Angry and rough around the ice and snow,
Calmly lapping on the tranquil golden shore,
Playful around the reefs and tickling the toddler's toes.

Tell me when you reach the end,
When you take the last look at the horizon and the setting sun,
When you venture around the world again,
So we can join to share and become one.

When You Said Your Last Goodbye
Hedley Richardson

A singing bird, a waving tree,
A happy time, just you and me.
A howling wind, a crashing sea,
By your side, wherever you may be.

You woke up with a tear drop in your eye,
I woke up next to you wondering why?
I am very worried, rather annoyed,
You stop speaking and start to avoid.

Something is wrong, not quite right,
You move away, we start to fight.
Which path do I follow? I am lost.
I cry an ocean and miss you lots.

When you whispered your last goodbye,
You left and you made me cry.
Being with you is the most treasured time,
I thought that you would always be mine.

Emotions of the Seasons
Alex Sands

Life is its own poem,
Full of choices and decisions to make,
With lots of emotions that it is bestowing,
There is only one path that you can take.

Poems can cause lots of emotions,
Whether happy, dull, jealous or sad,
They can tell you about fights and commotions,
That can make us angry and mad.

Autumn is enjoyable and winter is cold,
Seasons can spread emotions that make you reflect,
Spring is vibrant and summer is bold,
Emotions in seasons you can often detect.

So what path will you choose?
Will you be courageous every day and age …
Or will you be the one who is overwhelmed with rage.

A Mistaken World
George Taylor

From a push of just one button,
Sparks a digital world of joy.
Images, displayed with colour and meaning,
Websites full of items, begging and pleading.

An online bookstore, in which ignites reading.
However, you see
The internet doesn't always come with joy and glee.

People, just like you and me
Lurk in the depths, holding an unknown identity.
Maybe the people you talk to, hold records of theft and murder.

And if you still dare to explore further,
Your life maybe knocked over
And you will struggle to get back up, and may consider giving up.

For the internet is not a safe haven …
It's a gaping mouth that swallows the mistaken.

I Know That You Mean Well
Freddie Warburton

I know that you mean well,
Coming up to me with the hounds of hell,
The road to hell has good intentions to sell,
And when it sells it will ring its bells.

Another one is falling now,
When you see the devil you bow,
Then you will be thrown into a lava pit,
Your own inner demons come with a whip.

It's just you hurting yourself,
You staring back at you in the depths of hell,
Your mind creating a way to repent,
Going through this eternal torment.

You knew what you did was wrong,
It might not have taken too long,
You lived with it for the rest of your life,
And now you suffer eternal strife.

The Taunton Academy
Taunton – Somerset
Headteacher: Jenny Veal

End of the Year 1912
Thomas Hardy

You were here at his young beginning,
    You are not here at his aged end;
Off he coaxed you from Life's mad spinning,
    Lest you should see his form extend
        Shivering, sighing,
        Slowly dying,
    And a tear on him expend.

So it comes that we stand lonely
    In the star-lit avenue,
Dropping broken lipwords only,
    For we hear no songs from you,
        Such as flew here
        For the new year
    Once, while six bells swung thereto.

Eleven Year 10 students, sustained by Ms Rachael Logsdon, took part in the Thomas Hardy Poetry Workshop. They spent the day at Max Gate courtesy of the National Trust. They reported that they found the experience inspiring. They were particularly moved by visiting Emma's rooms upstairs. They asked many questions about Hardy's two marriages and felt that the house had 'reverberations of Emma'. They also fell in love with Hardy's study overlooking the garden. They all took part in lively readings of Hardy's and their own poems followed by intelligent discussions of both. They described the whole experience as 'evocative and really interesting'.

The Lonely Sunset
Callum Boyland

The peaceful yet powerful silence.
Deep in thought and not worry.
The dying sun still entranced
Be patient and watch, no need to hurry.

The birds rest and so do I.
Watching the dancing rays of orange and red
I'd rather stay here than go to bed.
Nobody to distract me, I wish there was.

Constantly alone like that star
Sparkling but still lonely
The wish for that one true love
Enters my dreams slowly.

Nobody cares, loves or wants me
Life can be cruel and unfair.
If only someone could see
And let me give them my love and care.

The Gift of Silence
Shannon Bradner

Silence ...
Just pure ... blissful ... silence ...
No shake, no stir ...
Only the graceful beauty of the surrounding world ...
Sublime within itself ...
Yet no figure to display such wonders.

But is everyone as privileged,
To receive such a blessing?
Or are the gentle wisps
Of mesmeric tranquillity
Sliced by intrusive demons
For others?

Here they sit ...
Quiet ... unsteady ...
Isolated and unwanted ...
So near to the edge.

Their broken heartstrings
Bleed the blues,
A melancholy cry amidst a world
Of seemingly salient woes.

Does silence ever truly penetrate
The loathsome screams of one's mind?
Or do the bitter thoughts,
Like knives in flesh,
Kill a silence
With a voice of its own?

Because Every Storm Cloud Has a Silver Lining
Elijah Chris

Bravest do it 'with a sword'
Cowards do 'it with a kiss'
The union who once stood
Look at your love
And what it has brought.

For it isn't peace or glory
But rather the true nature
Raw emotion and ugly tears
Suddenly there isn't a perfect picture

For the whispers of the night
Succumbed to the light
And the once happy giggles
Now mere secrets.

Rumours stir between the circles
Of princesses and dukes
With duchesses and archdukes.

In a world where those without power
Don't have a choice but to cower.

The money placed in your hand
And the crown lowered on to your head
Dictates your movements by hour
And enhances your elegance.

For the knight in shining armour
With Prince Charming from the tales
Makes your fall harder
When you notice the details.

cont ...

For his armour was shining
But it was bathed in innocent blood
And his smile might be charming
But it dragged your name through the mud.

For a girl like you
To fall in love with a guy like him
No can do.

But you taught us to be free.

And my darling you were a queen
Queens don't listen,
Queens bow before no man.

Why didn't you listen?

When he told you he didn't love you
All your bridges burned and hit the sea.

He loves me, he loves me not
Then a child's play.

Now your heart's been bought
And your world's all grey.

Nothing Left
Ella Gould

Cold stone mantel of
The once fiery grate.
Porcelain dogs
Upright, still,
Staring gold and emerald eyes.
Tarnished mirror
Reflecting memories,
Estranged faces staring back.

Musty rugs, long ago rich in
Jewelled threads.
Now stolen by troubled footsteps
Windows, cracked,
Smudged by deadened fingerprints,
Traced in dark, broken spider silk.
A bed bound in tight sheets.
Starched too stiffly long ago.

Cold places laid for one.
Nothing left today.

Dusk[1]
Charlotte Guns

Gold hour, here again;
I welcome it kindly – my old friend.
Crimson hues dance the sky
As the daylight begins to die.

My melancholy blues begin to play
As the sunlight fades away.

The reds and oranges leave in haste
As the blues and purples take their place.

The days in the sun are not over,
There is no need to give closure –
As the dawn will arrive again,
And I will welcome it – my old friend.

---

1   Note from poet: 'Thomas Hardy and Emma Hardy's relationship coming
to a close with Emma's death but how Thomas fell in love again with Florence.'

A Marriage Gone Wrong
Philippa Mannu

A marriage gone wrong,
or so he thought,
In death, true love's feelings were finally caught.

We question and ponder how this came to play,
How one's feelings could flip on such a dark day.

He inked his paper with words so true,
Incapable of paying attention to you.

You cook and you clean, trying to please,
Constantly saying 'this life comes with ease'.

But now I realise, behind the scenes,
This luxurious life is not all it seems.

Already Died
Destiny Pine-Brown

Without hope,
Without love,
When we got married,
We released a dove.

Now I'm trapped
In my room
Until the day,
I arrive at my tomb.

They say that when I was gone
He finally loved me.
His poems were sweet
Love letters even.

Shame I had already died.

The Window of Inspiration
Anya Wilson[2]

It changes the view ever so slightly,
But changes my perspective ever so mightily.
When the sun goes down, it casts a shadow over my view
But when the moon comes up it changes to something new.

When the rain runs down the vision is cloudy
But when a rainbow occurs I can write soundly.
I wish that she, the girl of my dreams,
Were alive as she seems.

So when I look out onto the court,
I forget the feelings I once sought,
I just wrote from my heart feeling inspired,
And found myself wondering if this is what we desired.

So when the sun comes out my writing is lifted,
But when the clouds go over it feels something has shifted
The shatters in the glass,
Shows thought and dreams that I thought once had passed.

---

2   Inspired by Emma's room.

Twilight
Christopher Wood

The orange sky blushed
Hues of pink and purple
As the day dies and the night starts
The land is glazed by a
Mysterious warmth.
A feeling of soothing serenity
Skims the tanned lustrous grasses
That have bathed in the Romantic
Summer evening glow as the
Sun finally fades giving room
For a newly birthed moon.
The ebb and flows of the
Summer grasses turn to the
Flowing swaying fields in the moonlight.
All of this in an hour
At twilight.

The Thomas Hardye School
Dorchester – Dorset
Headteacher: Mike Foley

The Wound
Thomas Hardy

I climbed to the crest,
And, fog-festooned,
The sun lay west
Like a crimson wound:

Like that wound of mind
Of which none knew,
For I'd given no sign
That it pierced me through.

Eleven Year 12 students participated in the Thomas Hardy Poetry Workshop. The day had a variety of activities including reading several Hardy poems, taking a long walk in search of inspiration, discussing Hardy and the art of composing poems and the students reading their own work. The walk was led by a student who took everyone towards a green landscape with a few trees. When asked what inspired them about the area, students pointed out two trees standing apart, a clump of trees to the left, a rigidly straight line of young trees to the side, an undulating landscape, the 'fake' exterior of Poundbury houses looking, in the students' words, 'like a clumsy theatre set with their unconvincing classical columns', a group of daffodils standing in rigid formation, the blue sky and the sunshine. A student gave an impromptu recitation of a favourite poem of his, 'A Poison Tree' by Blake. The evaluation of the day was positive. The students' sense of fulfilment was accurately reflected by a note received from a Sixth Form poet along with the poem e-mailed: 'Thank you so much for the insightful workshop. The way you look about the world has truly brought me peace of mind about my own future and how I may shape it into what I want it to look like.'

Collaborative Genius Interlude:

This poem was composed by the students after discussing their differing views on writing poetry.

Untitled Poem

you're short
you're gay
like a summer's day
the thunder laughed
and the ground shook
under my feet rubble started to move
I walked quickly the rubble between my toes
and skipped through the earth, away I go
I screamed as I fell down down down
the palpable blackness engulfed me
when I heard Theresa's drone again
I rushed at her with my poetic pen

'A square peg, being forced into a round hole'
Anonymous

But how can you blame me?

It would be unfair to call it a gruesome one,
But my life, has made me oh so 'square' ...

Morrisons, Bridport – a selection of differently flavoured tarts.
What was a sweet, sweet flavour
Turned to a bland mush.

He lay there on the cold bathroom tiles, asking for a friend of
his; of which, was not there.
Whilst I, with just my love keeping me going, helped my weak
father drink.
Lapsang Souchong. A tea I still drink to this day.
Holding back the tears (even now), my young self watched him
find the yin, to that moment's yang.

At a neighbour's house, just trying to get away and do what
children do, through a window
I see my aunt moving with haste and sincerity.
She barks how I must get home, straight away.

The house is desolate, silent – not what one expects from a
'standard' household.
A child lost in his own house.
I head up the teal stairs and into my parent's room.

There they all are:
Grandma, Mother, Brother and my Aunt.
In the middle:
Father.

cont ...

Young and innocent, but far from naïve,
I knew what was up.
This was it.
This time, the tears were plentiful.

With myself perched on the bed, we naturally form a circle
around him;
Whether or not he was conscious was not of concern.

"I love you dad. We love you."

As he passed and his body slumped, a luke warm moisture
engulfed my legs.
His internals finally had the opportunity to relax, once and for
all.
Uncharacteristic of a ten year old, no comments were made
until everyone was ready.
Ready to let go.

Two days later is my birthday, and it must be said:
They have never been the same since.

Now overlooking the countryside, where he lies
In peace.

The Field
Beatrice Bullough

The field sits like an ocean
Though it is not an ocean, but a field
For it is made of grass, not water
And in the flood, it's a shield.

The sun turns each blade to glass,
Each fractured shard is reflective.
The people don't care and despite this
Nature remains protective.

A thousand jewels, uncut and heavy,
Strewn around the Hawthorn trees
Diamond white yet bright with colour,
Priceless … yet free.

If only we knew, what we already do
That it crowns the ground, not the man,
Reflecting only the truth to us
Providing all that it can.

It is a field.

Nevertheless
Isobel Campbell

Hold breath tight
To fly to fight
To soar to fall
To win to lose
Let go
Nevertheless crash and relight,
Run far
Remember dreams
Dancers of the sky,
Moving clockworks
Collide
In unison in my eyes,
Re-entering
Reciting
Crashing lovingly,
The long forgotten
Lightning strikes
Thunder laughs
Ears alive,
Reach high
Grounded stay
Allow happiness
Rejuvenate hope
Nevertheless crash and relight,
Spark a fire
Search for a soul
Teach a brain
Reach a conclusion
Leave a judgement
Never too late
Never too early
Always the right time
Imagine reality
Allow illusions.
Nevertheless Crash and relight.

Picking up pieces
Emma Cuff

Sit next to me
Tell me now what you didn't back then
I won't mind,
Tell me what makes me so difficult to understand
I used to think you were everything I needed
How naive
To think I needed anyone but myself,
You broke me into millions of pieces
And I cried
Over the loss of myself and everything I believed
I cut myself on the broken pieces
Wished I could change
Until a light reached me
And I picked up the shards
And golden glue
And stuck the pieces into something new
And it's golden, warm, a hug from an old friend
Brave, strong, independent, resilient
So sit next to me
And I'll tell you what I didn't back then
I don't mind
Being difficult to understand.

Copacabana in October
Alice Cullinane

Walking down, sun rising around you,
With the sun, people wake, and start to move about,
Making my way to the seafront,
Watching the waves form and then
Crashing against the sand.
Like a heartbeat.
Regular.
In sync with life.
The ever-moving city blends to nothing,

Ha Long Bay
Alice Cullinane

Board the boat you'll be staying on for three days.
Come and look around.
The bathroom, with the broken tub.
The creaky floorboards.
The peeling paint on the windowpanes.
But outside is different.
Look around, see the green of the waves,
Watch as the fish swim in harmony,
See the jellyfish, floating as the tide pulls them.
But look up, the sky is sparkling. The sun is setting
Shades of fire pool out of the sky, molten, warm,
Thousands of colours surround you, a mosaic, a painting,
Dreams flutter around you, as stars in the sky
Seek knowledge, the secrets of the universe unfold
At your feet, and you are
Content.

The monster within
Alice Cullinane

It's always there.
A black cloud overlooking everything you do.
What you once loved, now feels grey
The voice inside, telling you you're not good enough.
You will fail when you aspire
You will fall when you climb
Just stop.

But there.
Just there
The murmur, the growing whisper,
The introduction of something unknown.
A way of control,
Over the uncontrollable.
You hear people telling you you've lost weight,
That you're not looking well
But you just smile and ignore,
You feel good.
But soon, that feeling is overpowered by something else,
Fear.
The fear of what you used to know.
You keep telling yourself
'I'm fine'

But with this ignorance
Comes the appointments
Comes the talking
Comes the waiting.
Waiting for comfort,
In death?
In recovery?
In life.

The 'O' Word
Molly Dunne

We don't mention the 'O' word
Not here, not in his house
For greater troubles are brought with it
Than what we need to fret about

A mouse might be seen as a nuisance
All covered in grey and white fur
But when our hair turns that colour
Our memories seem to blur

And wash over, like the waves
That brush against the shore
With all vigour and motion
That we possess no more

And people will say we're 'trouble'
They should have seen us as a child
The same cheeks, but now with lines
And a yellowed, gap-toothed smile

But all of these outer things
That our bodies have fallen into
Distracts us from the idea, the memory
We still laugh the way we used to

Yet still, they always ask
If we weren't always this grumpy
And if our bones weren't quite as stiff
Crooked, knotted, lumpy

cont ...

And now we are the roots
That ground the growing tree
That extends far past our own eyes
Forgetting the gnarled we

Our little legs would scale the heights
And fall upon the ground
And now our legs are full of wrinkles
Ridged, like our hands

We are climbed on, up and over
The saplings thirsting for sun
Even if time has won this war
We remember the child-like fun

But our eyes are still sharp
Our spirit, alive, and we cherish our aching bones
So there's no such thing as the 'O' word
No such thing, in this home

How Glad I'm Not in History
Joe Message

How glad I'm not in History,
How glad I'm here instead,
I'm sitting writing aimlessly,
But nothing's in my head.

On a thought's arrival,
work and commit to pen,
whatever spark I had in there,
before it's gone again.

A Night among the Stars
Lucas Miles

One summer's night we lay upon the grass,
Our thoughts whispering among the ageless stars,
Knowing this moment would come to pass,
Cold, wet, tired – unknowing of a light growing afar

A world just happening into my dimension,
Was engulfed by humble souls,
Disturbed by such meaningless expression,
Lingered on our faces.

A shy slip of exuberant red peaked over,
The light battling the beautiful darkness,
Holding us close till the promised dawn,
Releasing us from our perpetual silence.

Unnamed
Will Walden

I sat there alongside my friends,
With our individual minds and concerns,
Muddled in our heads.

A gentle breeze drifted through the reeds,
And tousled our hair as we perched and spectated.

In the near distance, branded trucks thundered without
noise along the motorway,
Scarring the land as it sliced through the serenity
Without causing disruption to our thoughts.

An ambiguous buzzing broke the silence
From somewhere in the grass.
An independent insect, trying to make its voice heard,
Even if it's only us who hear.

NoThInGs RiGhT WhEn It'S WrOnG
Michael Young

Nothing's right when it's wrong.
Nothing's right when grief is concealed,
locked away, starved of light and hungry
for hope. One summer seemingly cold, while
flowers freeze, pink dying roses placed
upon that single bed branded with death.
A stream of tears flowed rapidly from my face,
my Granny, my loving and caring life
just lay there, classical music playing gently by her place.
The room is an open coffin waiting to be closed,
yet I would stay trapped in motionless circles,
never to look beyond her dark corridor.
Before cancer ate her blessed corpse,
I was on holiday in Tenerife of course.
The tropical fruits of luxurious taste,
turned sour as soon as I left the place.
The pool of never eternal blue,
was stuck to me like glue.
The smell of the darker skies at night,
was sweetening, but not quite right.
Twelve hour shifts took my mind off gran's death,
but in the long run, grief never left.
When the darkest day seems clear and bright,
I know that it will never be right.
House now sold,
money now in,
justice will never be done.
Money exists, but grief's everlasting.
The smell of her clothes on that bed never goes,
despite my family washing her clothes.
I feel alone in a world full of noise,
where no one lives on, everyone dies, unknown
to the innocent children that play with their toys.
Nothing's right, when everything is wrong.

Trewirgie Junior School
Redruth – Cornwall
Headteacher: Jane Sargent

The Dream-Follower
Thomas Hardy

A dream of mine flew over the mead
　To the halls where my old Love reigns;
And it drew me on to follow its lead:
　And I stood at her window-panes;

And I saw but a thing of flesh and bone
　Speeding on to its cleft in the clay;
And my dream was scared, and expired on a moan,
　And I whitely hastened away.

Eleven Year 5 pupils, supported by Ms Mhairi Saville, took part in the Thomas Hardy Poetry Workshop. They responded to Hardy's poems in a variety of ways including engaging in discussions, replicating the rhythm and rhyme as a group, dancing to the rhythm, acting out any narrative within a poem and emulating Hardy's verses. They also took great delight in creating lines in a free-flow manner with each pupil contributing ideas and suggesting amendments. For example, one suggested that a first line could be 'He stares at me'; a second added 'She walked past me' as a second line. There were a lot of noisy discussions on how to promote and maintain the narrative in order to arrive at a last line simply stating, 'Now it is time to go ...'. These were impromptu lines that slowly morphed into the poems eventually written by each pupil. Evaluations were overwhelmingly positive and included: 'Hardy is a really good poet', 'This is enthusiastic learning', 'I enjoyed being a poem' (after some rôle play) and, probably most powerfully illustrative of the whole Workshop: 'Wow! What's left to explore after this?'

Group Poem

Pupils spent some time working as a group to create this poem. They composed group poems which were then performed through readings and, in two cases, through movement and dance. Each time that a poem was written, the group discussed it and made amendments as the majority saw fit. The young poets' focus was on the use of language within a narrative frame. They often sacrificed meaning for sonority, language and purposeful exuberance.

I

There is not much that I can do!
Below the bright light shines,
And the starry sky turns a beautiful blue,
And that is why I choose you
Every day I took out of the window and wonder ...
And go up a little bit yonder,
And a banana,
Man this is extravaganza,
The wonder is about the sky,
This is why I have to say bye
I can't write well but I have to try,
This is my final good bye.

II

Is there anything left for me to write about?
You could write about people doing good.
When they are doing more harm than good.
Like Columbus discovering a happy family,
Having a blast on the beach collecting shells.
When the gifts he brought were deadly diseases.

cont ...

III

'Good morning! Good morning!' said he.
As he rushed by with horse and carriage.
He gazed out at the beautiful twinkling river
He then looked at the sky.
It was a deep blue colour, which made him cry but why?
Because it's snowing.
The banana I was going to dumb is frozen and going
And up it goes up the tree slowing
To thee who goes to me
Will always be by my side,
And will never leave me alone.

IV

He stares at me,
She walked past me.
My name was once Bob but it's now Oscar.
Old Grandad won the Lottery.
Suddenly the banana grew legs and arms and fell free and ripe,
The banana tripped over and knocked a tree over.
Soon the weirdo married the banana
Then the animals had a baby called Jeff and
He wanted to be a princess when he was
Older, it was not possible though because
He was a boy and his parents didn't like princesses.
Four animals were together and they were going into the blue lake,
Mmm … I love sharks I like their crunchiness
That's the best animal to me tasty and bees are lovely
Now it's time to go.

An August Midnight
Allissia Anson

A bright light, a rumbling wind,
One moth ready to soar,
A buzz from a phone,
A trip to the stars,
The moth is on his way.

I thought to myself above all more,
What could be on that phone, so sore,
The moth comes closer and closer I find,
Then what was originally in my mind,

Then I wonder to myself,
The moth is god's love,
From all the way up above.

A Childhood Memory
Mia Bickford

I don't want to look away,
I want these memories to stay,
But these memories keep ageing day by day,
And pushing me further away.

I remember the day,
When we all played on the beach in our holiday,
Meanwhile Mum sunbathed away.

Or when me and Brother went to Gran's stables,
To feed the horses their hay.

But now those memories are fading away,
And they will never come back and stay.

A bright window
Jack Bolt

A bright window and a flappy curtain,
Will scare the little moth for certain,
The moth flies at it at 40,
And the window said no that's naughty,
And an Italian bloke,
Will surely give the moth a wing that's broke,
"Ouch that hurt" the moth spoke,
He took his last flap and sped into the light,
For the moth's final fight.

The child of memory
Oscar Bolt

I can't look away,
But it's another day,
So it's gone away,
And why did I crave,
To what I have to wave.

She went to where,
As I do not dare,
So why to care of there,
Where I first learnt to share.

That is the sign,
I can mime,
When I could rhyme,
And not commit a crime.

The Moth
Oscar Chown

A light in the shape of a square
Gives everyone except a scare
It says there clutching the warmth
Every person gets a taunt
And this is a fact
It stays there until it falls on its back
At this point of time at this point of space
It will stay there in that very place
But not for a second are they dumb
As the moth knows more about the earth than everyone.

The Night of the Insects
Harry Dyer

A bright phone and a blinding light,
With a moth a fly and a longlegs on this Tuesday night,
The humble moth repeatedly ramming in to the lamp,
The fly is crawling on the old Gramp,
The longlegs is just being big,
Whilst the fly is hiding under a wig,
How they're still awake at this late hour,
Is a thing called insect power!!!

When I was young
Mia Gray

These are my memories,
Looking up my childhood
I looked in the mirror and that was me,
Being young was great,
Like being young and eight,
I don't want to forget so I look in the sky,
But I know I have to say bye.

Standing on the old floor,
Creaky, old and thin,
Here was the living room,
And here was my bed
Memory's going by around my mind,
This is where I was kind,
Now it's been too long I have to go say goodbye,
So these are my final farewells and byes.

Memories
Morwenna Halloway

Here are the creaky stairs,
Worn out by playing.
Lego still places I never dreamed of,
My mum by the fire

The chimera spitting out sparks
   The B.B.Q. dying out
   The big dipper watching over
The smoke as thick as a blanket

Like I am hypnotised
I stared into the centre of the fire
My crazy dog on my lap
The other on my feet

Childhood
Fynn Johns

Here is my favourite floor,
It used to be my only floor,
I used to look forward to school,
I used to like being so cool,
We used to play a game of man hunt,
And if I won I would kick a punt,
I faintly remember spending a pound,
On my family's very own ground,
I used to play on my saxophone,
And my mum used to let out a groan,
I used to plant my own flower,
So I guess this is child power.

Childhood Memories
Mina Kellow

Looking up at the moonlit sky,
I realise I don't want the memories to go,
But this is how I have to say goodbye,
Even though it's where I had my first snow,
Memories flashing through my mind,
This is where I learnt to be kind,
Although it's not the perfect place,
It always felt like a safe place,
But now it's my final bye,
Farewell now and goodbye.

A Moth's Life

Alma Luke

A bright computer and a blinding light,
Gives the little moth a great big fright,
He flies away, sad, scared and worried,
He then escapes, and off he scurried,
At 700 miles an hour,
The moth sped into a flower,
He exclaimed, "Oi! Look where you're going!",
He said as the river was flowing,
The flower replied, "Not my fault, mate!",
The moth replied, "Don't hate!",
Then the river exclaimed so loud,
"Shhhh, be quiet," she scowled,
"Who cares!" said the rude moth,
As he fell into a bowl of broth,
"Ewww! Potatoes in my ears!",
That was one of moth's biggest fears!

Afterword

Logs on the Hearth   *A Memory of a Sister*
Thomas Hardy

The fire advances along the log
    Of the tree we felled,
Which bloomed and bore striped apples by the peck
Till its last hour of bearing knelled.

The fork that first my hand would reach
    And then my foot
In climbings upward inch by inch, lies now
Sawn sapless, darkening with soot.

Where the bark chars is where, one year,
    It was pruned, and bled –
Then overgrew the wound. But now, at last,
Its growings all have stagnated.

My fellow-climber rises dim
    From her chilly grave –
Just as she was, her foot near mine on the bending limb,
Laughing, her young brown hand awave.

Appendix 1 below is the booklet used with the students during each Thomas Hardy Poetry Workshop. It is reproduced here precisely as the students received it, hence the different font.

Appendix 2 gives the 'Thomas Hardy Workshop Plans' which were used in each school. Depending on students' responses to the poetry of Thomas Hardy, there were only minor adjustments to the 'Plans' made where necessary.

The basic approach remained largely unchanged. It included starting off with an open and broad discussion of reading and writing poetry. This was followed with readings of Thomas Hardy's ten selected poems.

Discussions of the Hardy poems read were encouraged with a series of questions listed in the 'Plans' in Appendix 2. Students were asked to emulate a favourite poem.

Finally, students wrote their own poems inspired by reading Hardy and sharing their work amongst the group. Each time that a student read his/her poem, listeners were asked to give positive responses first with evidence from the text followed by one or two areas for improvement that might be of help to the aspiring poets.

This brief Introduction will focus solely on reporting the students' responses to Thomas Hardy's poetry.

Participating students shared the following ten poems by Thomas Hardy:

An August Midnight
The Self-Unseeing
The Orphaned Old Maid
The Fiddler
A Church Romance
When I Set out for Lyonnesse
Beeny Cliff
A Poet
At the Railway Station, Upway
On a Discovered Curl of Hair

The most popular poems were 'An August Midnight', 'The Self-Unseen', 'A Church Romance', 'A Poet' and 'At the Railway Station, Upway'.

Amongst the principles agreed on writing poetry was the one stating that 'there is no good poetry or bad poetry: there is only self-expression within a free and mutually supportive group'. A second principle agreed upon was that 'composing a poem could be quite artificial, e.g. occasional poetry on "demand"'. Occasional poems by past Poet Laureates were shared, e.g. Tennyson's 'The Charge of the Light Brigade' or Carol Ann Duffy's 'The Wound in Time'. The aim was to give students confidence in their own ability to express themselves and to respect their poetic outcomes. Consequently, students were able to decide for themselves what they wished to write and how they wished to write it.

In one school, students wanted to spend some time 'rewriting' Hardy's 'An August Midnight' – by far the most popular poem amongst the students who took part in the Thomas Hardy Poetry Workshops.

The outcomes showed clear understanding of Hardy's poem, of its structure, rhythm, rhymes and intent. Taking Hardy's opening lines, the Greenwood Academy students wrote:

'An electric light flickers and curtains sway,
Television noises coming from the living room,
A knock at the door and my mom comes in …' (Phoebe McFarlane)

'A dusty lamp and the aroma of ancient books
The sounds of a video game from the cooks
On this scene enter misery, disgusting and dirty …' (Jessica-Jayne Lucas)

'A loud TV and a broken lamp
And the loud voices of my parents.
On this scene enter – devil horned, evil …' (Molly Selby)

Hardy's style is borrowed and his vision adopted to portray the individual young poet's world of today. His message of humility and empathy remains as seen in these Greenwood Academy concluding lines:

'There the spider gently strolls onto my hand.
I release the creature back into mother nature's arms.' (Charlie Wattis)

Or, Hardy's last two lines are adapted to represent the young poet's anger at today's rabid capitalism:

'I muse about what to buy. Yet why?
Why waste time over trivial things?' (Phoebe McFarlane)

Or, Hardy's conclusion is used to illustrate arrogance by reversing Hardy's portrayal of humility:

'Humans are the top creature
These insects need not feature.' (Alastair Hill-Weddle)

This pattern of adopting, amending and borrowing from Hardy was fairly consistently used by students as a first step towards writing their own poems for this Anthology. Thomas Hardy is first emulated and then used as the inspiration for the students' own creative outpourings, as shown by this poem composed by Lewis Carr of Greenwood Academy:

A dusty lamp and a political revolution,
And the screams of social media from a distance:
At this instance enter – death, war and salvation.
A starving child, a broken country and heavy silence.
While mid thought stands a broken world
That traps its people in suspense ...

Face to face with these three nefarious topics,
My mind melts into a solitary pool of hope;
Hope that all these children get fed, hope that:
Broken countries become one again,
Hope that the silence of the world's fear are
Released and desperately demolished. At once.

Many students wrote poems recognisably based on Hardy's works. 'The Self-Unseeing' inspired poems by many students in the Greenwood Academy: Lewis Carr, Ana Cristea, Chanel Hill, Jessica-Jayne Lucas, Alicia Madaleno, Phoebe McFarlane, Charlotte Parkes, Romany Taylor Bartlett, Wajia Timar, Bethany Tracey, Abigail-Naomi Turnbull and Charlie Wattis. Some students from St Osmund's also based their poems on 'The Self-Unseeing': Hedley Richardson and Freddie Warburton. So did some Trewirgie pupils: Mia Bickford, Mia Gray, Morwenna Halloway, Fynn Johns, Mina Kellow and Alma Luke. Hardy's poem also inspired Ruby Barker of St Ives School to write about childhood memories.

Scarlett McMahon from St Ives based her poem 'Romancing the Church' on Hardy's 'A Church Romance'.

The highly popular 'An August Midnight' inspired similar poems from Bryanston School students Serena Forwood, Eliza Harwood and Nicole Liou, as it did from Trewirgie pupils Allissia Anson, Jack Bolt, Harry Dyer and Alma Luke. St Ives students collaborated on composing their own 'An August Midnight'. Hedley Richardson of St Osmund's Church of England Middle School composed 'When You Said Your Last Goodbye' with its echoes of Hardy's 'An August Midnight'. Alex Way's Cape Cornwall poem 'In 2020' has reverberations of Hardy in its style and message.

Hardy's poem 'The Orphaned Old Maid' inspired one poet who wished to remain anonymous from St Osmund's Church of England Middle School to compose 'Silence is the Answer and Nameless is the Price'.

Leah Turner's 'When we first met' has recognisable echoes of Hardy's 'When I set out for Lyonnesse'.

Although not taking part in the Thomas Hardy Poetry Workshops, Kitty Fisher, a student in Year 9 at Colyton Grammar School, composed the poem 'Reading "A Wife in London"'. Her wonderful poem was a perfect example of how students could produce beautiful pieces inspired by Thomas Hardy. Kitty Fisher's poem won the National Trust Thomas Hardy Young Poetry Prize 2019. The runner up and all the Highly Commended were students from the Thomas Hardye School (although only one, Alice Padgett, had actually taken part in the Thomas Hardy Poetry Workshops).

The majority of young poets wrote poems inspired by reading Hardy's ten poems (or only some of them depending on the time available). Many students' poems have a clearly perceived link to a Hardy poem, as shown above. Others were prompted by discussions of his poetry which led the students to have a go and 'do their own thing'.

The poems presented here are all precisely as they were written by the young poets. No amendments or corrections were made. Where there may be apparent 'error' or eccentric punctuation or mode of expression, these were checked with the poet and were then published exactly as s/he wanted. Taking liberties with the use of extreme poetic licence was a third agreed underlying principle of all the Workshops.

As interludes were needed, the young poets took part in one of the following two light-hearted verse 'games': (1) Exquisite Corpses: They had a first line of a poem written on a piece of paper. The paper was passed on to a student who wrote a second line. Before s/he passed the paper on to the next student, s/he bent it so that the first line could not be seen and the next writer saw only the previous line just written. The third writer wrote a line continuing the second line and bent the paper so that his/her line was the only one that could be seen by the fourth writer, and so on. At the end of the process the paper returned to the one who had written the first line. A student read the finished poem out. Participants discussed the poem to determine whether it made sense, was cohesive, and so on. The group edited the poem to 'improve' it. (2) Collaborative Genius: A first line was written and the paper was passed on without hiding any previous writing. As the paper went around the room, each student added one line, and so on. The paper came back to the first writer who then read it out. A discussion similar to that for (1) above took place.

Students consistently reported back on their enjoyment of reading Hardy's poems. A few suggested that they would have liked to look at similar themes in poems written by other nineteenth-century poets. They were promised that future sessions would include poems by Romantic poets whose influence on Hardy's writings would make comparing and contrasting 'similar' poems a little easier for participating students.

The following are a few of the participants' evaluations: 'the teacher is funny', 'enjoyable', 'free to express myself', 'analysis of the poems gave me ideas', 'loved the "no wrong answers" idea', 'the group poem was fun', 'I really enjoyed changing Hardy's old poem', 'my favourite was rewriting the Lyonnesse poem', 'great discussions', 'I enjoyed the critical friend bit', 'Thomas Hardy is a really good poet', 'I like expressing my thoughts', 'the teacher is really enthusiastic', 'pleasant to listen to each other', '"The Self-Unseeing" made me want to be a child again but this time I am looking', '"The Self-Unseeing" shows that anything can happen in a child's world', 'the teacher's passion for poetry is infectious', 'can we have more lessons like this next year?', 'it is fantastic to be able to re-write the Greats', 'this was real fun', 'the teacher was a bit crazy whenever he read our poems – really cool', 'I really enjoyed expressing myself'.

Perhaps the biggest tribute paid to these poetry sessions was one reluctant student who quietly said: 'I've never been a great fan of poetry. Now, I feel that I'm a real poet'.

Another student said: 'Today's world desperately needs poetry … I will continue to write in order to make sense of our current chaos!'

Students from the Taunton Academy spent the day at Max Gate. Their evaluation showed the impact of being in the 'presence' of Hardy, Emma and Florence: 'Stories about Hardy and his wives were deeply touching', 'reading Hardy in his house felt wonderful', 'the in-depth reading of Hardy's poems in the very room where he might have written them was fantastic', 'the tour of Max Gate was great'.

Many parents commented positively and generously about their children's experiences of the Thomas Hardy Poetry Workshops. A parent said that the students 'raved about the session' and that the day was 'the most positive experience they have had in recent months'.

The youngest participants were Year 5 children whose evaluations were remarkably mature: 'Wow! What's left to explore after this?', 'in "An August Midnight" Hardy shows us that every creature, no matter how little, is an important part of our world', 'reading "The Self-Unseeing" gives me a sense of regret and makes me want to enjoy being a child because anything can happen in a child's mind'.

In his Preface to *Poems of the Past and the Present* Hardy writes that the poems comprised 'a series of feelings and fancies written down in widely different moods and circumstances, and at various dates' which might show that they possessed 'little cohesion, thought or harmony of colouring'. He adds, 'Unadjusted impressions have their value, and the road to a true philosophy of life seems to lie in humbly recording diverse readings of its phenomena as they are forced upon us by chance and change'.

This little book shows the young poets' very diversity of impressions that Thomas Hardy speaks of here. It gives young poets the chance to write in 'widely different moods and circumstances' and, yet, with apparent 'cohesion of thought' and 'harmony of colouring'.

Perhaps the last word should go to a Sixth Former who wrote: 'I just want to take this opportunity to thank you for doing this Workshop. This is the first poetry I have ever written and not only have I enjoyed the process but I feel real accomplishment as a writer. I hope you continue the sessions so others can enjoy the experience too'.

Faysal Mikdadi
Academic Director of The Thomas Hardy Society
Dorchester
July 2019

Appendix 1

THE THOMAS HARDY SOCIETY

c/o Dorset County Museum, Dorchester, Dorset DT1 1XA
01305 251 501 info@hardysociety.org www.hardysociety.org

School Poetry Workshop

Contents

13 An August Midnight[1]

I

A shaded lamp and a waving blind,
And the beat of a clock from a distant floor:
On this scene enter – winged, horned, and spined –
A longlegs, a moth, and a dumbledore;   *dumbeldore: bumblebee*
While 'mid my page there idly stands
A sleepy fly, that rubs its hands ...

II

Thus meet we five, in this still place,
At this point of time, at this point in space.
– My guests besmear my new-penned line,   *besmear: smear over/stain*
Or bang at the lamp and fall supine.   *supine: lazily inactive/listless*
'God's humblest, they!' I muse. Yet why?
They know Earth-secrets that know not I.
Max Gate, 1899

Notes[2]
*'Hardy's reverence for all life had some basis in his reading in science, in
evolutionary theory, all living things are akin ....' Hardy once remarked: '"I
often wonder how much animals know – about things – things of which we
are 'ignorant'." The "Earth secrets" that he supposed the insects might know
are not earth's meanings. They do not know more than the poet does, but each
perceives something the other does not.'*

---

1   The figure in front of the title of each poem is the number of the poem
in *Thomas Hardy: The Complete Poems*, Edited by James Gibson, Palgrave
Macmillan, first published in 1976.
2   Notes are based on *The Poetry of Thomas Hardy – A Handbook and
Commentary* by J. O. Bailey, The University of North Carolina Press, Chapel
Hill, USA, 1970.

135 The Self-Unseeing

Here is the ancient floor,
Footworn and hollowed and thin,
Here was the former door
Where the dead feet walked in.

She sat here in her chair,
Smiling into the fire;
He who played stood there,
Bowing it higher and higher.

Childlike, I danced in a dream;
Blessings emblazoned that day;   *emblazoned: displayed brightly*
Everything glowed with a gleam;
Yet we were looking away!

Notes
This poem *'presents Hardy's nostalgic meditation during a visit to his boyhood home at Higher Bockhampton ... The characters are himself, his father, and his mother'*. Hardy as a child was no more than four years old dancing to his father's playing of the violin.

203 The Orphaned Old Maid

I wanted to marry, but father said, 'No –
'Tis weakness in women to give themselves so;
If you care for your freedom you'll listen to me,
Make a spouse in your pocket, and let the men be.'   *spouse: husband*

I spake on't again and again: father cried,
'Why – if you go husbanding, where shall I bide?   *bide: live/dwell*
For never a home's for me elsewhere than here!'
And I yielded; for father had ever been dear.

But now father's gone, and I feel growing old,
And I'm lonely and poor in this house on the wold,   *wold: an area bare*
And my sweetheart that was found a partner elsewhere,   *of woods/high*
And nobody flings me a thought or a care.   *rolling country*

Notes
'... *a monologue in the speech of a country woman.*'

207 The Fiddler

The fiddler knows what's brewing   *fiddler: violin player*
   To the lilt of his lyric wiles: *wiles: tricks to deceive*
The fiddler knows what rueing   *rue: regret/sorrow*
   Will come of this night's smiles!

He sees couples join them for dancing,
   And afterwards joining for life,
He sees them pay high for their prancing
   By a welter of wedded strife.   *welter: confusion*

He twangs: 'Music hails from the devil,
   Though vaunted to come from heaven,
For it makes people do at a revel
   What multiplies sins by seven.

'There's many a heart now mangled,
   And waiting its time to go,
Whose tendrils were first entangled   *tendrils: threads that*
   By my sweet viol and bow!'   *hold a plant together*

Notes

This poem *'expresses a fiddler's half-rueful exultation in his power to stir dancing couples to emotional madness'*. The music has such an effect on the listeners that they get carried away, fall in love and marry – only to discover their rash mistake later on.

211 A Church Romance

(*Mellstock* circa *1835*)

She turned in the high pew, until her sight
Swept the west gallery, and caught its row
Of music-men with viol, book, and bow
Against the sinking sad tower-window light.

She turned again; and in her pride's despite
One strenuous viol's inspirer seemed to throw
A message from his string to her below,
Which said: 'I claim thee as my own forthright!'

Thus their hearts' bond began, in due time signed.
And long years thence, when Age had scared Romance,
At some old attitude of his or glance
That gallery-scene would break upon her mind,
With him as minstrel, ardent, young, and trim,   minstrel: singer or musician
Bowing 'New Sabbath' or 'Mount Ephraim.'

Notes

This poem tells the story of Thomas Hardy's parents' first meeting in their local church. The poet's grandfather *'led the choir at Stinsford Church, playing the 'cello. The other instrumentalists were his sons, Thomas and James ...This choir performed twice each Sunday in the now-demolished West Gallery of the Church'.*

254 When I Set out for Lyonnesse

(1870)

When I set out for Lyonnesse,   *Lyonnesse: Cornwall*
  A hundred miles away,
  The rime was on the spray,   *rime: white frost, hoarfrost*
And starlight lit my lonesomeness
When I set out for Lyonnesse
  A hundred miles away.

What would bechance at Lyonnesse   *bechance: happen, befall, happen to*
  While I should sojourn there   *sojourn: stay for a short time*
  No prophet durst declare,   *durst: dared*
Nor did the wisest wizard guess
What would bechance at Lyonnesse
  While I should sojourn there.

When I came back from Lyonnesse
  With magic in my eyes,
  All marked with mute surmise   *surmise: guess*
My radiance rare and fathomless,
When I came back from Lyonnesse
  With magic in my eyes!

Notes

This is *'a lyric record of Hardy's first trip to St Juliot in Cornwall on March 7, 1870, his falling in love with Emma Lavinia Gifford, and his return to Higher Bockhampton with "magic" in his eyes'.*

291 Beeny Cliff

March 1870–March 1913

I

O the opal and the sapphire of that wandering western sea,
And the woman riding high above with bright hair flapping free –
The woman whom I loved so, and who loyally loved me.

II

The pale mews plained below us, and the waves seemed far away   *nether:*
In a nether sky, engrossed in saying their ceaseless babbling say,   *lower*
As we laughed light-heartedly aloft on that clear-sunned March day.

III

A little cloud then cloaked us, and there flew an irised rain,
And the Atlantic dyed its levels with a dull misfeatured stain,
And then the sun burst out again, and purples prinked the main.   *prink:*

dress for show

IV

– Still in all its chasmal beauty bulks old Beeny to the sky,   *chasm: gap*
And shall she and I not go there once again now March is nigh,
And the sweet things said in that March say anew there by and by?

V

What if still in chasmal beauty looms that wild weird western shore,
The woman now is – elsewhere– whom the ambling pony bore,
And nor knows nor cares for Beeny, and will laugh there nevermore.

Notes

'Beeny Cliff has two dates below the title, March, 1870, and March, 1913. They indicate the fusion of two visions of the cliff as Hardy saw it when he was taken there by Emma Gifford on his first visit and when he returned alone after her death.' The 'woman riding high above' is Emma. 'Beeny Cliff is often covered in mists that give the sea below a slate-blue color[3]; sea-birds circle and call below the crest. In sunlight, underwater rocks color the water with rainbow colors. Hardy's description in the poem is accurate.'

---

3   J. O. Bailey uses the American spelling of 'color' (rather than the British spelling of 'colour').

336 A Poet

Attentive eyes, fantastic heed,
Assessing minds, he does not need,
Nor urgent writs to sup or dine,   *i.e. invitations to dine*
Nor pledges in the rosy wine.   *i.e. toasting his health with wine*

For loud acclaim he does not care
By the august or rich or fair,
Nor for mart pilgrims from afar,
Curious ın where his hauntings are.   *i.e. visitors after a celebrity*

But soon or later, when you hear
That he has doffed this wrinkled gear,   *i.e. he has died*
Some evening, at the first star-ray,
Come to his graveside, pause and say:

'Whatever his message – glad or grim –
Two bright-souled women clave to him.'   *clave: clung/stuck to*
Stand and say that while day decays;
It will be word enough of praise.
July 1914

Notes

'*A Poet* seems Hardy's suggestion for his epitaph. In July, 1914, he had been
married to Florence Dugdale only five months, but he knew that, at seventy-
four, he might not live much longer, and that [his poetry book] Satires of
Circumstance *might be his last volume ....*' The reference to 'two bright-souled
women' may be to his two wives Emma Gifford and Florence Dugdale. Bailey
reports that '*Lois Deacon expressed to me the opinion that, though Hardy
wished his readers to identify the women as Emma and Florence, "bright-
souled" does not accurately describe either of them, and that Hardy had in
mind his mother Jemima and his early sweetheart Tryphena Sparks. Tryphena
did not "cleave" to him.*'

563 At the Railway Station, Upway

'There is not much that I can do,
　　For I've no money that's quite my own!'
　　Spoke up the pitying child –
A little boy with a violin
At the station before the train came in, –
'But I can play my fiddle to you,
And a nice one 'tis, and good in tone!'

The man in the handcuffs smiled;
The constable looked, and he smiled, too,
　　As the fiddle began to twang;
And the man in the handcuffs suddenly sang
　　With grimful glee:　　　　　　　*grimful: frightful/not yielding*
　　'This life so free
　　Is the thing for me!'
And the constable smiled, and said no word,
As if unconscious of what he heard;
And so they went on till the train came in –
The convict, and boy with the violin.

Notes
*'"Upway" for Upwey, a village on the River Wey about three and half miles
south of Dorchester ... The prisoner is probably being taken to Portland Prison
on the Isle of Portland.'*

630 On a Discovered Curl of Hair

When your soft welcomings were said,
This curl was waving on your head,
And when we walked where breakers dinned   *dinned: made a loud noise*
It sported in the sun and wind,
And when I had won your words of grace
It brushed and clung about my face.
Then, to abate the misery
Of absentness, you gave it me.

Where are its fellows now? Ah, they
For brightest brown have donned a gray,
And gone into a caverned ark,   *i.e. into a grave*
Ever unopened, always dark!

Yet this one curl, untouched of time,
Beams with live brown as in its prime,
So that it seems I even could now
Restore it to the living brow
By bearing down the western road
Till I had reached your old abode.
February 1913

Notes
This poem *'describes a lock of hair contained in a green leather locket with a miniature of Hardy's first wife Emma ... The poem is a soliloquy* [talking to oneself/speaking out one's inner thoughts to no one in particular] *addressed to Emma's spirit three months after her death when Hardy had "discovered" the curl of hair and returned in memory to his courtship.'*

Appendix 2

The Thomas Hardy Poetry Workshop Plans

Academic Committee Members: Dr Tracy Hayes, Andrew Hewitt, Dr Karin Koehler, Dr Jonathan Memel, Dr Faysal Mikdadi, Andrew and Marilyn Leah.

- Lead the students in a general discussion on reading and writing poetry, including, where feasible, working in small groups or in pairs and reporting back to the whole group.
- The aims of this session are:

✓ To engage with students within a relaxed and friendly ambience.
✓ To elicit from students an acknowledgement of having read and written poems.
✓ To get students to talk about favourite poems read.
✓ To encourage students to discuss their own writing (of verse or prose).
✓ To get students to talk about what inspires them to write.
✓ Where possible, to get students to talk about a favourite poem including ones learnt in childhood.
✓ To imbue students with a sense of worth: their views of poetry in particular and writing in general are sought, appreciated and respected.
✓ To engage reluctant students.
✓ To discuss how poems are composed.
✓ To show that writing poetry is both an art form as well as a formulaic process that could be engaged with through inspiration and, often, without.
✓ To suggest that a few Thomas Hardy poems are shared as exemplars worthy of emulation.

The booklet put together includes ten Thomas Hardy poems:
An August Midnight
The Self-Unseeing
The Orphaned Old Maid
The Fiddler
A Church Romance
When I Set out for Lyonesse
Beeny Cliff
A Poet

At the Railway Station, Upway
On a Discovered Curl of Hair

- Engage the students in a conversation on poetry. Should there be any reluctant participant, introduce examples of creative work other than writing. Students may talk about their drawings, paintings, designing and making, music compositions and playing, singing, dancing, etc. Try to find the students' 'inner spark of divine fire' to share and celebrate in order to validate the individual student's self-worth.
- Explain how poems are written, e.g. when the poet is experiencing an overwhelming emotion, after a significant event, on seeing something inspiring, etc. Most importantly, explain that, for now, there is no good poetry or bad poetry: there is only self-expression within a free and mutually supportive group.
- Explain that composing a poem can be quite artificial, e.g. occasional poetry on 'demand'. Maybe read one or two such poems by Poet Laureates, e.g. Tennyson's 'The Charge of the Light Brigade' or Carol Ann Duffy's 'The Wound in Time' on the occasion of the Armistice Day Centenary. Argue that beautiful, evocative and memorable poems have been written on demand to celebrate an occasion or an event.
- Ask the students to suggest an occasion worthy of versification. Choose one or two suggestions, dramatically ask for silence, shut your eyes and throw out a few lines improvised on the spot. Ask them to help you by suggesting further lines. Write all that is suggested and, in a few minutes, stop the activity and read the resultant short poem. Discuss the poem. Give students the opportunity to rewrite the poem in any way that they see fit. Ask them to give reasons for the suggested amendments.
- Read a selection of the poems listed. How many poems one should read will be determined by the students' responses. Read the first poem. Students are gently urged to volunteer to read subsequent poems. Where needed, readers are given advice on how to read confidently and how to declaim.
- After a poem is read, suggest that when reading a poem there are two things that we are looking for: (1) immediate meanings or events; and (2) deeper meanings. For example, after reading 'An August Midnight', the following questions on item (1) above are asked: (a) Where is the poet in this narrative? (In his study.) (b) What is he doing? (Writing.) (c) Who or what comes in? (Four creatures/insects.) (d) What is the fly doing? (Rubbing its hands.) (e) What happens to the poet's page of writing? (The ink is smudged.) The students should be praised for understanding the 'events' of the poem. Now, the following questions on item (2) above are asked:

(a) What do you think the poet is trying to tell us? (A little observation or vignette of something that happened late at night in his study.) (b) Can you support your response with a quotation from the poem? (He describes the light and sounds in the room and then tells us 'On this scene enter ...'. (c) What does the poet think that these four creatures are to start with? ('God's humblest, they!') (d) When he changes his mind, what does he think about these creatures? ('They know Earth-secrets that know not I.')

- Give the students a chance to expand on their understanding of the poem in any way. Encourage them to use the few 'Notes' given in the booklet provided to the participants.

- Ask the students, working alone or in pairs, to replace the first six lines of the poem with their own observation of anything that comes to their mind. They can, if they wish, use Hardy's language if they need to, e.g. they can write, 'An old desk lamp and a dusty blind, / And the sound of mum's TV the other side of my wall: / On this scene enter – fluttering, mewing, and growling / My horrible brother, with his I-Phone and grumpy mood ...'. The lines need not rhyme.

- The process is repeated with other poems. As each poem is read, discussed, analysed and 're-written', students are encouraged to take risks and 'improve' on Hardy using their own poetic genius. Seek variety from the students and encourage different approaches, ideas, expressions, forms, structures and styles.

- As interludes are needed, stop the process and introduce one of the following two light-hearted verse 'games': (1) Exquisite Corpses: Write a first line of a poem. Pass the paper to a student who writes a second line. Before s/he passes the paper on to the next student, s/he bends the paper so that the first line cannot be seen and the next writer sees only the previous line just written. The third writer writes a line continuing the second line and bends the paper so that his/her line is the only one that can be seen by the fourth writer, and so on. At the end of the process the paper returns to the one who had written the first line. Read the finished poem out. Ask one or more students to re-read the poem to everyone. Encourage a discussion on whether the poem makes sense, is cohesive, and so on. As a group, the poem may be edited to 'improve' it. (2) Collaborative Genius: A first line is written and the paper is passed on without hiding any previous writing. As the paper goes around the room, each student adds one line, and so on. The paper comes back to the first writer who then reads it out. A discussion similar to that for (1) above takes place.

- During breaks, seek out reluctant participants and engage them in discussions on any subject that emerges naturally. Encourage them to talk freely and praise their responses. Suggest that you and others would be really interested in hearing their views on poetry and ask them to consider reading a poem when the group gets back together after the break.

- Ask the following questions before moving on to the next Thomas Hardy poem: (1) Do poems have to make sense? (2) Do poems have to rhyme? (3) What matters more: the meaning or the sound? (4) How long or short should a poem be? (5) What possible poetic devices can the students think of (with examples where possible)?
- Share further Thomas Hardy poems. As each discussion takes place, begin to ask more subtle questions and to look for deeper meanings.
- The students can have between thirty minutes and one hour to compose their own individual poems. On some rare occasions, two close friends may collaborate on writing a single poem. Students may produce whatever they wish. If they need a framework or writing scaffold, they may use any Thomas Hardy poem from the little booklet, emulate it or, if they feel the need, borrow from it (ask the students doing so to ensure that what they borrow is clearly placed within inverted commas to acknowledge that the words are not theirs – explain why this should always be done).
- Once the writing session is over, each student is encouraged to read his/ her work to the others. After each reading, students are asked to give only positive comments to start with. Whatever comment they make, they should be challenged to offer evidence from the text. After all the positive comments are made, students are asked to be critical friends and to suggest what could be done better (always with clear reference to the text being critically appreciated).
- After the whole session is over, the students' poems are word processed, printed and displayed in public areas around the school or published in small school anthologies. Students able or willing to do so should be encouraged to read their poems at school-based events both to their peers, their family and to the local community. Their poems should be entered into as many competitions as may be available for the students' various age ranges.